Speed, Agility and Quickness for CRICKET

SAQ ® Cricket

Alan Pearson

A & C Black • London

Metric to Imperial conversions

1 centimetre (cm)	=	0.394 in
1 metre (m)	=	1.094 yd
1 kilometre (km)	=	1093.6 yd
1 kilogram (kg)	=	2.205 lb

First published 2004 by A&C Black Publishers Ltd
37 Soho Square, London W1D 3QZ
www.acblack.com

Copyright © 2004 by SAQ International Ltd

ISBN 0 7136 6376 6

Acknowledgements
Cover photograph courtesy of EMPICS; all other photographs courtesy of SAQ International; illustrations courtesy of Angus Nicol.

Typeset in Photina
Printed and bound in Great Britain
by Biddles Ltd, King's Lynn

Speed, Agility & Quickness International Limited Trade mark numbers:

'SAQ' ® Britain and Northern Ireland No. 2156613
'SAQ' ® European Community No. 001026277
'SAQ Speed, Agility, Quickness' ® Australia

SAQ ™

SAQ Programmes™
SAQ Equipment™
SAQ Training™
SAQ Accreditation Awards™

In addition to the above, the following trademarks are in current commercial use by SAQ International and have been for several years in respect to their products and services:

Fast Foot™ Ladder
Viper Belt™
SAQ Continuum™
Jelly Balls™
Micro Hurdles™
Macro Hurdles™
Speed Resistor™
Sprint Sled™
Power Harness™
Sonic Chute™
Agility Disc™
Side Strike®
Flexi-cord™
Velocity Builder™
Heel Lifter™
Visual Acuity Ring™
Peripheral Vision Stick™
Break Away Belt™ and Tri-Break Away Belt™
Dynamic Flex®
Bunt Bat™

Discover more about SAQ Programmes, SAQ Accreditation Awards and SAQ Equipment online at www.saqinternational.com

Contents

Acknowledgements

I would like to thank Dave Whatmore for introducing me and the Programme to Lancashire CC in the mid nineties. His enthusiasm and support helped the SAQ Programme take off within the United Kingdom. A very special thank you to one of the best cricketers in the UK to have not yet been capped for his country, Steffan Jones. Working together, our goal was to make him bowl faster than ever before. It was fantastic watching him win a one-day final at Lords, taking four wickets and bowling at over 91 mph. A special thank you to Keith Fletcher, Roni Irani, Grahame Gooch, Jamie Foster and the players and staff that I have met at Essex CC. They have been great fun to work with, receptive to new ideas and also very professional and committed to success on the field. Thanks to Ron Cochrane and Duncan Hall of Brisbane, Australia. Thanks to Joe Shepherd, Allan Dilly of the Loughborough University Cricket Academy, and also the academy players James Adams, Paul Carter, Marc Rosenberg and David Wigley. Also a big thank you to Marcus Trescothick.

The illustrations in this book have been produced by Stephen Gilbert, whose attention to detail and incredible computer skills have made this book the best SAQ one so far. Finally, a big thanks to Rebecca Parrott for her administrative support and to all the SAQ staff, and love to my supportive wife, Silvana.

Alan Pearson,
May 2004

Foreword

Speed, agility, quickness and multi-directional explosion are key components of the physical demands required of a cricket player. All aspects of cricket, including fielding, bowling, batting and wicketkeeping, require the ability to move with incredible speed, power and precision. The SAQ Programme has been implemented by Essex County Cricket for over 5 years. Not only is it effective, it is also challenging and motivational for players who have not only enjoyed but have also benefitted from this new approach to training and conditioning for Cricket. Alan Pearson's position-specific and practical approach to cricket, which is scientifically based yet delivered in a simple, effective manner, makes it suitable for all cricketers from amateurs to seasoned internationals. I would encourage all coaches to read this most informative book and introduce the concept and drills to their training regime.

Graham Gooch, Essex CC, England, International Player, Captain, Coach, England Selector

Since the cricket revolution of the late seventies and early eighties, the game of cricket at all levels has evolved into a dynamic contest. Many aspects of the game are about the ability of the players to rapidly decelerate, redirect and accelerate as well achieving high speed.

How does the coach increase the athletic performance of his players to respond to the challenges of the game in the twenty-first century? The answer to this question is akin to most innovations in sports coaching, that is, necessity is the mother of invention.

The innovative approach of the SAQ method of warm-up and the development of cricket skills throughout the activity sets in this book will enhance the ability of the team, the individual and the coach. Coaches who adopt the SAQ approach to their cricket coaching will be the lighthouse coaches for the next generation.

Ron Cochrane, Director of Sport, Brisbane Grammar School Australia Australian Level 3 Accredited Coach CA 400305 Member of the Development Team for the Australian Institute of Sport Cricket Academy

I was introduced to Alan Pearson and SAQ over five years ago and my goal was to bowl as fast as possible. I introduced SAQ principles to my training and conditioning programme and, with Alan's ongoing support, over a period of time I increased my bowling speed by 10mph. Not only was the programme effective, it was challenging, interesting and, due to the variations and progressions, it was enjoyable. I believe that the SAQ Cricket Book is one of the most important training and conditioning tools in the world of cricket. I recommend it to all coaches and players, whatever age and standard.

Steffan Jones, Somerset CC, Northampton CC and Wales

I started working with SAQ with my playing colleague Steffan Jones. I found that the training made sense and was more related to the cricket-specific movements required while playing the game.

I found the training effective, hard work but enjoyable. The SAQ Book is full of great training ideas that will improve all cricketers' fitness and ability to play the great game.

Marcus Trescothick, Opening Batsman,
Somerset CC and England

As a wicketkeeper, multi directional explosive speed and reactions are a crucial part of my game. I have been using SAQ for a number of years, both with Essex County Cricket and Durham University CC. The drills and the equipment make you feel explosive, therefore I use SAQ on a regular basis throughout the season. To all wicketkeepers, I can recommend the SAQ Cricket Book.

Jamie Foster, Essex CC and England

Introduction

THE FOUNDATION OF SAQ CRICKET

Cricket is one of the most widely played sports in the world and is enjoyed by players of all ages, both male and female. Much has been written about the wonderful game of cricket with many famous writers alluding to the game's grace, gentlemanly conduct and skill. Yet cricket is the most explosive game played in the world. There is nothing more exhilarating, dynamic and intimidating than a fast bowler accelerating to the delivery crease and firing a ball at nearly 90 mph; the incredible reactions and agility of a slips fielder diving full length to catch a ball travelling at an incredible speed, one-handed, to take a match-winning catch; the amazing hand, eye and foot co-ordination, anticipation and fine motor skills of a batsman, who with incredible control hits a ball in the centre of the bat and drives it to the cover boundary for four runs. Cricket has all these wonderful ingredients. These superb acts of speed, agility and quickness are what make the difference between winning and losing at whatever level the game is played. Often thought by many to be god-given gifts, and therefore neglected on the training field, such abilities are admired and believed to be essential for success within the game by coaches, trainers, selectors and players. Cricket is a very athletic game, therefore it is crucial that speed, agility and explosive acceleration are trained for and practised.

The SAQ Cricket Programme is the first ever cricket-specific training conditioning programme that focuses on the key areas of speed, agility and quickness. The programme also has other significant benefits such as reduction in injuries and improvement in visual awareness skills, hand and foot co-ordination, strength and core control as well as being full of variety, challenging and fun for all players. The programme has been developed over many years working with international and county coaches and players from around the world. The secret lies in the SAQ Continuum and the use of progressive sequential learning techniques, breaking down complex sports science and making it easy to understand and practical to use. The SAQ Continuum caters for long-term athletic development and multi-skilled training. The end result is the development of multi-directional explosive speed specifically for the cricketer. This unique programme can be adapted to meet the needs of all ages and can be used for both team and individual training within a squad that requires position-specific development. The programme also provides an excellent opportunity for coaches and trainers to develop new skills and drills, thus increasing their professionalism.

This book enables coaches, trainers, selectors and players to understand how and why SAQ Programmes work. It provides clear, precise examples on how to put theory into practice on the training ground. Its progressive structure even covers position-specific drills and allows SAQ training to be integrated into all cricket training sessions.

What is SAQ Training?

Speed has long been considered as just a matter of how fast an object can go from point A to point B; only recently has it been studied and broken down into stages such as acceleration, the 'planing-out' phase, deceleration, etc. Much of this research has been carried out by sports coaches involved in straight-line running, so that the jumping, turning and zigzagging speed necessary in cricket has been somewhat neglected.

Those involved with the development of SAQ Programmes have sought to fill this void so as to develop all types of speed, particularly for team sports such as cricket. SAQ Programmes break speed down into three main areas of skill: speed, agility and quickness. Although these may appear to be similar they are in fact quite different in terms of how they are trained, developed and integrated into a player's performance. When these skills are successfully combined and specialist SAQ Equipment is utilised, they provide the coach with the tools to turn a good player into an outstanding one. It is remarkable what players can achieve with an SAQ Programme.

Speed

A crucial part of any player's game is the ability to cover the ground efficiently and economically over the first few yards and then to open up stride length and increase stride frequency when working over 40–50 yards. Speed means the maximum velocity a player can achieve and maintain. In most humans the ability to maintain this maximum velocity is for a short period of time and distance only. Speed can also be measured by the amount of time it takes a player to cover a particular distance.

Training to improve maximum speed requires a great deal of focus on correct running mechanics, stride length and frequency, the leg cycle and hip height/position. Drills such as the 'dead-leg run' and stride frequency drills that are used to help develop an economical running technique can all be easily integrated into a training session.

The best sprinters spend very little time in contact with the ground and what contact they do make is extremely efficient and powerful. Focusing on the mechanics of running helps to control and use this power efficiently and sparingly. Training when fresh is also crucial for an athlete/player to attain maximum speed. Many athletes can only reproduce top speeds for a few weeks of the year but the inclusion and practise of correct running mechanics on the training field will bring great benefit. How often have you seen a cricket player run as if he or she is also playing a kettledrum, that is, with poor arm mechanics? Such a running style will have a detrimental effect on the overall performance and, importantly, the speed of the player.

Agility

Agility is the ability to change direction without the loss of balance, strength, speed or body control. There is a direct link between improved agility and the development of an individual's timing, rhythm and movement.

Agility should not be taken for granted and can actually be taught to individual players. Training ensures that a cricket player develops the best offensive and defensive skills possible with the greatest quickness, speed and control and the least amount of wasted energy and movement. Agility also has many other benefits for the individual, helping to prevent niggling injuries and teaching the muscles how to fire properly and control minute shifts in ankle, knee, hip, back, shoulder and neck joints for the optimum body alignment.

Another very important benefit is that agility training is long-lasting. Unlike speed, stamina and weight training, it does not have to be maintained to retain the benefits. Consider the elderly person who can still ride a bicycle 40 years after having last ridden one. Agility training acts like an indelible mark, programming muscle memory.

THE FOUR ELEMENTS OF AGILITY

There are four elements to agility:

- Balance
- Co-ordination

- Programmed agility

- Random agility

Within these there is speed, strength, timing and rhythm.

Balance is a foundation of athleticism. Here we teach the ability to stand, stop and walk by focusing on the centre of gravity; balance can be taught and retained relatively quickly. Examples include: standing on one leg, walking on a balance beam, standing on a balance beam, standing on an agility disc, walking backwards with your eyes closed and jumping on a mini trampoline and then freezing. It does not take too long to train balance. It requires only a couple of minutes, two or three times a week and should be done early in the morning and early in a training session.

Balance is complicated by additional stresses. **Co-ordination** is the goal of mastering simple skills under more difficult stresses. Co-ordination work is often slow and methodical, with an emphasis on correct biomechanics during athletically demanding movements. Training co-ordination can be achieved by breaking a skill down into sections then gradually bringing them together. Co-ordination activities include footwork drills, tumbling, rolling and jumping. More difficult examples are: walking on a balance beam while playing catch, running along a line while a partner lightly pulls and pushes in an attempt to move the player off the line and jumping on and off an agility disc while holding a jelly ball.

The third element of agility training is called **programmed agility**. This involves a player who has already experienced the skill or stress that is to be placed on him or her and is aware of the pattern and sequence of demands of that experience. In short, the player has already been programmed. Programmed agility drills can be conducted at high speeds but must be learnt at low, controlled speeds. Examples are zigzag marker drills, shuttle runs and T marker drills, all of which involve changes of direction along a known standardised pattern. There is no spontaneity.

Once these types of drills are learnt and performed on a regular basis, times and performances will improve and advances in strength, explosion, flexibility and body control will be witnessed. This is true of players of any ability.

The final element, the most difficult to master, prepare for and perform, is **random agility**. Here the player performs tasks with unknown patterns and unknown demands. Here the coach can incorporate visual and audible reactive skills so that the player has to make split-second decisions with movements based upon the various stimuli. The skill level is now becoming much closer to that of actual game situations. Random agility can be trained by games of tag, various ball-games and more specific training such as jumping and landing followed by an immediate unexpected movement demand from the coach.

Agility training is challenging, fun and exciting. There is the opportunity for tremendous variety and training should not become boring or laborious. Agility is not just for those with elite sporting abilities – try navigating through a busy shopping mall.

Quickness

When a player accelerates, a great deal of force has to be generated and transferred through the foot to the ground. This action is similar to that of rolling a towel up (the 'leg'), holding one end in your hand and flicking it out to achieve a cracking noise from the other end (the 'foot'). The act of acceleration in a fraction of a second takes the body from a static position to motion. Muscles actually lengthen and then shorten instantaneously – that is an 'eccentric' followed by a 'concentric' contraction. This process is known as the stretch shortening cycle action (SCC). SAQ Training concentrates on improving the neuromuscular system that impacts on this process, so that this initial movement – whether lateral, linear or vertical – is automatic, explosive and precise. The reaction time is the time it takes for the brain to receive and respond to a stimulus by sending a message to the muscle causing it to contract. This is what helps a cricket player to cut right – left – right again and then burn down the sideline. With ongoing SAQ Training, the neuromuscular system is reprogrammed and restrictive mental blocks and thresholds are removed. Consequently, messages from the brain have a clear path to the muscles, and the result is an instinctively quicker player.

Quickness training begins with 'innervation' (isolated fast contractions of an individual joint), for example repeating the same explosive movement over a short period of time, such as fast feet and line drills. These quick, repetitive motions take the body through the gears, moving it in a co-ordinated manner to develop speed. Integrating quickness training throughout the year by using fast feet and reaction-type drills will result in the muscles having increased firing rates, which creates players capable of faster, more controlled acceleration. The goal is to ensure that your players explode over the first 3–5 yards. Imagine that the firing between the nervous system and the muscles are the gears in a car; the timing, speed and smoothness of the gear change means the wheels and thus the car accelerate away efficiently, with balance and co-ordination, so that the wheels do not spin and the car does not lose control.

Movement Skills

Many elements of balance and co-ordination involve the processing of sensory information from within the body. Proprioceptors are sensors that detect muscular tension, tension in tendons, relative tension and pressure in the skin. In addition, the body has a range of other sensors that detect balance. The ability to express balance and co-ordination is highly dependent on the effectiveness of the body's internal sensors and proprioceptors, just like the suspension on a car. Through training, these sensors, and the neural communication system within the body, become more able to interpret external information and formulate the appropriate movement response. This physiological development underpins effective movement and future movement skill development.

SAQ Equipment

SAQ Equipment adds variety and stimulus to your training session. Drill variations are unlimited and, once mastered, the results achieved can be quite astonishing. Players of all ages and abilities enjoy the challenges presented to them when training with SAQ Equipment, particularly when introduced in a cricket-specific manner.

When using SAQ Equipment, coaches, trainers and players must be aware of the safety issues involved and of the reduced effectiveness and potentially dangerous consequence of using in-appropriate or inferior equipment.

The following pages introduce a variety of SAQ Equipment recommended for use in many of the drills detailed later in this book.

FAST FOOT LADDERS

These are made of webbing with round, hard plastic rungs spaced approximately 18 inches apart; they come in sets of two pieces each measuring 15 feet. The pieces can be joined together or used as two separate ladders; they can also be folded over to create different angles for players to perform drills on. Fast Foot Ladders are excellent for improving agility and for the development of explosive fast feet.

MICRO AND MACRO V HURDLES

These come in two sizes: Micro V Hurdles measuring 7 inches and Macro V Hurdles measuring 12 inches in height. They are constructed of a hard plastic and have been specifically designed as a safe freestanding piece of equipment. It is recommended that the hurdles be used in sets of 6–8 to perform the mechanics drills detailed later. They are ideal for practising running mechanics and low-impact plyometrics. The Micro V Hurdles are also good for lateral work.

SONIC CHUTE

This is made from webbing (the belt), nylon cord and a lightweight cloth 'chute', the size of which may vary from 5 to 6 feet. The belt has a release mechanism that, when pulled, drops the chute so that the player can explode forwards. Sonic Chutes are excellent for developing sprint endurance.

VIPER BELT

This is a resistance belt specially made for high-intensity training. It has three stainless steel anchor points where a flexi-cord can be attached. The flexi-cord is made from surgical tubing with a specific elongation. The Viper Belt has a safety belt and safety fasteners; it is double stitched and provides a good level of resistance. This piece of equipment is useful for developing explosive speed in all directions.

SIDE-STEPPERS

These are padded ankle straps that are connected by an adjustable flexi-cord. They are useful for the development of lateral movements.

REACTOR

A rubber ball specifically shaped so that it bounces in unpredictable directions.

OVERSPEED TOW-ROPE

This is made up of two belts and a 50-yard nylon cord pulley system. It can be used to provide resistance and is specifically designed for the development of express overspeed and swerve running.

BREAK-AWAY BELT

This is a webbing belt that is connected by Velcro-covered strips. It is good for mirror drills and position-specific marking drills, breaking apart when one player gets away from the other.

STRIDE FREQUENCY CANES

Plastic, 4-foot canes of different colours that are used to mark out stride patterns.

SPRINT SLED

A metal sled with a centre area to accommodate different weights and a running harness that is attached by webbing straps of 8–20 yards in length.

JELLY BALLS

Round, soft rubber balls filled with a water-based jelly-like substance. They come in different weights from 4 to 18 lb. They differ from the old-fashioned medicine balls because they can be bounced with great force onto hard surfaces.

HANDWEIGHTS

Foam-covered weights of 1.5–2.5 lb. They are safe and easy to use both indoors and out.

VISUAL ACUITY RING

A hard plastic ring of approximately 30 inches in diameter with four different-coloured balls attached to it, all equally distributed around the ring. The ring helps to develop visual acuity and tracking skills when thrown and caught between the players.

PERIPHERAL VISION STICK

The stick is simple but very effective for the training of peripheral vision. It is approximately 4 feet long with a brightly coloured ball at one end.

BUNT BAT

A 4-foot stick with three coloured balls – one at each end and one in the middle. Working in pairs, Player 1 holds the bat with two hands while Player 2 throws a small ball or bean bag for Player 1 to 'bunt' or fend off. This is effective for all players and particularly so for hand–eye co-ordination.

AGILITY DISC

An inflatable rubber disc 18 inches across. The discs are multi-purpose but particularly good for proprioreceptive and core development work (to strengthen the deep muscles of the trunk). They can be stood on, knelt on, sat on and lain on for the performance of all types of drills.

SIDESTRIKE

A heavy-duty platform with raised angled ends for foot placement. The ends are adjustable to accommodate different size athletes, and the surface is padded to provide protection. It is an excellent piece of equipment for explosive foot-work development, ideal for goalkeepers, cricketers and tennis players.

The SAQ Continuum

Many games activities are characterised by explosive movements, acceleration and deceleration, agility, turning ability and speed of responses (Smythe 2000). The SAQ Continuum is the sequence and progression of components that make up an SAQ Training session. The progressive elements include cricket-specific patterns of running and drills including ball work. The Continuum is also flexible, and once the pre-season foundation work has been completed and the season has begun, when time and recovery are of the essence short combination SAQ Training sessions provide a constant top-up to the skills that have already been learned.

SAQ Training is like any other fitness training – if neglected, then players' explosive multi-directional power will diminish. The component parts of the SAQ Continuum and how they relate to cricket are:

- **Dynamic Flex** – warm-up on the move
- **Mechanics of movement** – the development of running form for cricket
- **Innervation** – fast feet, agility and control for cricket
- **Accumulation of potential** – the bringing together of the previous components in an SAQ Training cricket circuit
- **Explosion** – the development of explosive 3-step multi-directional acceleration for cricket
- **Expression of potential** – short competitive team games that prepare the players for the next level of training
- **Warm-down**

Throughout the continuum, position-specific drills and skills can be implemented.

CHAPTER 1 DYNAMIC FLEX

WARM-UP ON THE MOVE

It is common knowledge that before engaging in intense or strenuous exercise the body should be prepared. The warm-up should achieve a change in a number of physiological responses in order that the body can work safely and effectively:

- increased body temperature, specifically core (deep) muscle temperature

- increased heart rate and blood flow

- increased breathing rate

- increased elasticity of muscular tissues

- activated mental alertness.

The warm-up should take a performer from a rested state to the physiological state required for participation in the session that is to follow. The warm-up should gradually increase in intensity as the session goes on. In addition it should be fun and stimulating for the players, switching them on mentally.

The standard training session for cricket begins by warming the players up either by jogging around the outfield or performing a short catching or fielding drill, then taking them through a series of static stretches that focus on the main muscle groups in the body. However, static stretches are not only irrelevant within the game of cricket but are more likely to cause injury and loss of power (Kokkonen, Nelson and Cornwell, 1998). Cricket players do not need to be able to do the splits like gymnasts and dancers, but they need to be able to perform dynamic movements of catching, fielding, diving, bowling and hitting the ball at all angles around the ground. Dynamic Flex is what allows the cricket player to do this: flexibility in action, if you like, combined with power, strength and control. You do not pull a muscle standing still, so how do you warm it up statically?

Indeed the most recent research has shown that static stretching before training or competitions can actually be detrimental to performance. Rosenbaum and Hennig (1995) document that static stretching resulted in peak force reduction: 5 per cent reduction in rate of force production and an 8 per cent decrease in Achilles tendon reflex activity; Oberg (1993) states that static stretching resulted in a decrease in torque during eccentric contractions; Bennett (1999) claims that pre-exercise static stretches decreased eccentric strength by 9 per cent for up to one hour.

The eccentric strength of the muscle is its ability to apply force when lengthening, for instance when an opening bowler lands then applies the brakes immediately after a delivery – his or her ability would typically be reduced by up to 9 per cent for up to an hour after static stretching. Sadly, we still see bowlers performing static stretches not only before the start of the game but just prior to their spell of bowling. Recently a national newspaper reported that 13 English international pace bowlers have been injured in one 12-month period, and three of the top-ranked medium-pace bowlers have been injured in the same period, taking the total to 15 in one year. One of the main arguments in favour of static stretching has been that it helps to prevent injury and muscle soreness. Once again the latest research suggests the opposite. Gleim and McHugh (1997) state that it is not possible to draw any relationship between flexibility and the risk of injury. Pope (1999) concluded that there was no difference in the occurrence of injury between army recruits who stretched and those who did not. Herbert and Gabriel (2002) suggest that stretching before exercising does not seem to confer a practically useful reduction in the risk of injury. The effects of static stretching on Delayed Onset of Muscle Soreness (DOMS) is inconclusive and the research on this matter is very limited. Smith et al. (1993) report that static stretching leads to a higher level of DOMS than not stretching. Herbert and Gabriel (2002) say that 'stretching before or after exercise does not confer protection from muscle soreness'. Getting muscle soreness after physical activity is natural. After a period of time with continued activity the body will adapt and cope with the soreness.

The reliance on long, slow, steady-state running to develop endurance for cricketers is also another major factor in causing soft tissue injuries brought on by repetitive movements; the running required for cricket is explosive and therefore utilises fast-twitch not slow-twitch fibres . This will be discussed in the endurance running section later in this book.

The Warm-up

Using a standard 22 × 22 yard grid, the following exercises represent a foundation set of Dynamic Flex warm-up drills. Also included in this chapter are variations and the introduction of the ball.

It is important to remember that cricket players not only enjoy variety but also that they respond proactively on the field to the variations training. Once they have mastered the standard set the introduction of new grids and combination work including the ball will ensure maximum participation.

> In a warm-up drill, start slowly, rehearse the movements then increase the intensity.

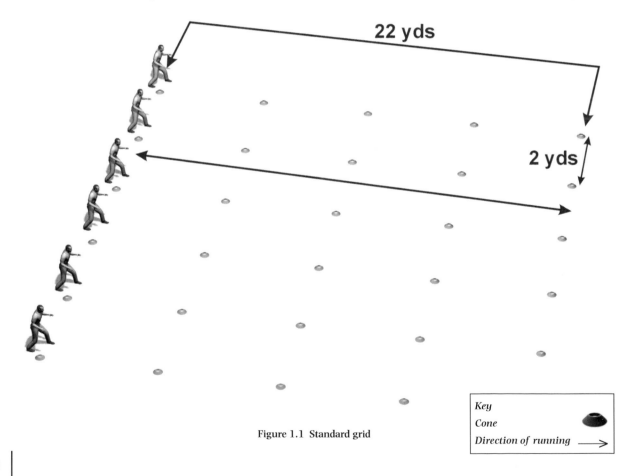

22 yds

2 yds

Figure 1.1 Standard grid

Key
Cone
Direction of running ⟶

DRILL ARM ROLL AND JOG

Aim
To improve shoulder mobility, balance and co-ordination, to increase body temperature and to develop positive foot-to-ground contact.

Area/equipment
An indoor or outdoor grid 22 yards in length. The width of the grid is variable depending on the size of the group. One cricket ball per player.

Description
Player covers length of grid by jogging forwards and backwards, rolling the arms forwards so that they move from below the waist to above the head in a rolling motion.

Ball
The ball is held in one hand as the arm is rotated, then swapped over and held in the other hand for the return.

Key teaching points
- Keep the arms slightly bent
- Keep off the heels
- Maintain an upright posture
- Ensure adequate spacing between players

What you might see
- Arms too far to the horizontal
- Torso sunk into the hips

Solutions
- Brush arms past ears in a more vertical rotational movement
- Breathe in and out lightly, hold contraction so that normal breathing can occur

Sets and reps
2 × 22 yards, 1 forwards and 1 backwards.

Variations/progressions
Perform the drill laterally.

DRILL SPOTTY DOGS

Aim
To improve shoulder and arm mobility, activate core muscles, improve balance and co-ordination and increase body temperature.

Area/equipment
An indoor or outdoor grid 22 yards in length. The width of the grid is variable depending on the size of the group. One cricket ball per player.

Description
Player covers length of grid by simultaneously chopping the legs and arms out, left leg to left arm, right leg to right arm. Range of movement for the arm is from the side of the body up to the side of the face.

Balls
The ball is held out in one hand as the arm is pushed out, then swapped over and held in the other hand for the return.

Key teaching points
- Keep off the heels
- Arm action is a chop not a punch
- Land and take off on the balls of the feet
- Maintain an upright posture
- Keep the head up

What you might see	Solutions
Players landing flat-footed	Ensure the players work on the balls of the feet by getting them to lean slightly forwards
Jerky, unbalanced movements, poor co-ordination	Develop a rhythm by getting the players to call 'out, in, out, in' while they perform the drill; the calls are to coincide with movement of the legs and arms

Sets and reps
2 × 22 yards forwards.

Variations/progressions
Players can perform the drill using opposite arms to legs.

DRILL *JOG AND HUG*

Aim
To improve shoulder and chest mobility, balance and co-ordination and to increase body temperature.

Area/equipment
An indoor or outdoor grid 22 yards in length. The width of the grid is variable depending on the size of the group. One cricket ball per player.

Description
Player covers the length of the grid by slowly jogging, bringing both arms around the front of the body so that fingers can grip behind the opposite shoulder. Alternate the arms over and under.

Ball
The ball is held in one hand as the arm is squeezed around the front of the body, then swapped over and held in the other hand when the arms are changed.

Key teaching points
- Squeeze slowly
- Ensure adequate spacing between players
- Jog on the balls of the feet
- Maintain an upright posture

What you might see
- Trunk held too upright

- Running on the heels

Solutions
- Tilt trunk slightly forwards, drop chin down closer to chest
- Lean body forwards; this will push weight onto the balls of the feet

Sets and reps
2 × 22 yards forwards.

Variations/progressions
Squeeze and then rotate the core turning from left to right, right to left.

DRILL | STAR JUMPS

Aim
To improve shoulder mobility, balance and co-ordination. To develop positive foot-to-ground contact.

Area/equipment
An indoor or outdoor grid 22 yards in length. The width of the grid is variable depending on the size of the group.

Description
Player performs drill on the spot simultaneously bringing arms out and above the head so that the insides of the arms are nearly touching the ears and the hands come together above the head. The legs are split out in a jumping movement then brought together at the same time as the arms are brought back to the sides.

Ball
The ball is held in one hand as the arm is raised for the first 10 jumps, then swapped to the other hand for the last 10 jumps.

Key teaching points
- Develop a rhythm
- Do not sink into the hips
- Stay tall
- Land and take off on the balls of the feet and not on the heels
- Ensure adequate spacing between players

What you might see	Solutions
Torso sinking into the hips on landing	Breathe in–out, breathe in again, and hold the contraction so as to breathe comfortably while performing the drill
Deep bending of the knees on landing	Players to land on the balls of the feet with firm knees that give only slightly

Sets and reps
20 star jumps.

Variations/progressions
Alternate basic drill with bringing the arms out above the front of the head; then alternate with bringing the arms out above the side of the head.

DRILL   WALKING ON THE BALLS OF THE FEET

Aim
To stretch shins and improve ankle mobility. To improve balance and co-ordination. To increase body temperature.

Area/equipment
An indoor or outdoor grid 22 yards in length. The width of the grid is variable depending on the size of the group.

Description
Player covers the length of the grid by walking on the balls of the feet, and returns to the start by repeating the drill backwards while handling the ball.

Ball
The ball is tossed from hand to hand just below head height while the drill is carried out.

Key teaching points
- Do not walk on the toes
- Keep off the heels
- Maintain correct arm mechanics
- Maintain an upright posture
- Squeeze buttocks together

What you might see
- Players walk on toes

- Legs too wide apart

Solutions
- Players to focus on walking on the balls of the feet, keeping the head horizontal and with the body leaning slightly forwards
- Feet should be shoulder-width apart; use marker dots for spacing if necessary

Sets and reps
2 × 22 yards, 1 forwards and 1 backwards.

Variations/progressions
Players to perform drill with arms stretched out above the head; this will challenge balance and core control.

DRILL LATERAL WALKING ON THE BALLS OF THE FEE

Aim
To stretch shins and improve ankle mobility. To improve lateral balance and co-ordination. To increase body temperature.

Area/equipment
An indoor or outdoor grid 22 yards in length. The width of the grid is variable depending on the size of the group.

Description
Player covers the length of the grid by walking on the balls of the feet sideways, then returns to the start by repeating the drill moving in the opposite sideways direction.

Ball
The ball is tossed from hand to hand just below head height while the drill is carried out.

Key teaching points
- Do not bring the feet completely together
- Do not cross the feet
- Do not walk on the toes
- Keep off the heels
- Maintain correct arm mechanics
- Maintain an upright posture
- Keep the hips square
- Feet to be shoulder-width apart
- Keep the head up in an upright posture

What you might see
- Crossing of feet
- Loss of balance
- Strides too long

- Bringing the feet together

Solutions
- Keep hips square
- Drop heels to just above surface
- Work with feet shoulder-width apart

- Work with feet shoulder-width apart

Sets and reps
2 × 22 yards, 1 leading with the left shoulder and 1 with the right.

Variations/progressions
Hold the arms above the head.

DRILL ANKLE FLICKS

Aim
To stretch calves and improve ankle mobility. To improve balance, co-ordination and rhythm of movement. To prepare for good foot-to-floor contact. To increase body temperature.

Area/equipment
An indoor or outdoor grid 22 yards in length. The width of the grid is variable depending on the size of the group.

Description
Player covers the length of the grid in a skipping motion where the balls of the feet plant then flick up towards the shin, moving in a rhythmic, bouncing manner. Return to the start by repeating the drill backwards.

Ball
The ball should be rotated around the body at waist height. Alternate from left to right, then from right to left.

Key teaching points
- Work off the balls of the feet, not the toes
- Practise the first few steps on the spot before moving off
- Maintain correct arm mechanics
- Maintain an upright posture

What you might see
- Poor plantar-dorsiflex range of movement (raising and lowering of the toes)
- Jerky, unrhythmic movement

Solutions
- Players should pull toes towards shin on the upward flick
- Use calls 'up, down' or 'one, two' to help with rhythm

Sets and reps
2 × 22 yards, 1 forwards and 1 backwards.

Variations/progressions
Perform the drill laterally.

DRILL SMALL SKIPS

Aim
To improve lower leg flexibility and ankle mobility. To improve balance, co-ordination and rhythm and to develop positive foot-to-ground contact. To increase body temperature.

Area/equipment
An indoor or outdoor grid 22 yards in length. The width of the grid is variable depending on the size of the group.

Description
Player covers the length of the grid in a low skipping motion, and returns to the start by repeating the drill backwards.

Ball
The ball to be repeatedly tossed at approximately head height.

Key teaching points
- Raise knee to an angle of about 45–55 degrees
- Work off the ball of the foot
- Maintain correct arm mechanics
- Maintain an upright posture
- Maintain a good rhythm

What you might see
- Knee lift too high

- Poor rhythm

Solutions
- Player to focus on the knee not coming any higher than the waistband
- Same as above

Sets and reps
2 × 22 yards, 1 forwards and 1 backwards.

Variations/progressions
Perform the drill laterally.

DRILL   KNEE-OUT SKIPS

Aim
To stretch the inner thigh and improve hip mobility. To develop an angled knee drive, balance, co-ordination and rhythm. To increase body temperature.

Area/equipment
An indoor or outdoor grid 22 yards in length. The width of the grid is variable depending on the size of the group.

Description
Player covers the length of the grid in a skipping motion. The knee moves from the centre of the body to a position outside the body before returning to the central position. Return to the start by repeating the drill backwards. The ball is to be used as a target for the knee.

Ball
The hand is held out at an angle and the knee is brought up to touch the ball, then the ball is transferred to the other hand and the movement repeated on the other side.

Key teaching points
■ Feet start in a linear position and move outwards as the knee is raised
■ Work off the balls of the feet
■ The knee is to be pushed, not rolled, out and back
■ Maintain correct arm mechanics
■ The movement should be smooth, not jerky

What you might see	Solutions
■ Landing on the heel	■ Focus on landing on the balls of the feet, trunk leaning forward
■ Leaning back too far	■ Keep head slightly dipped towards chest

Sets and reps
2 × 22 yards, 1 forwards and 1 backwards.

Variations/progressions
Perform the drill laterally.

DRILL SINGLE-KNEE DEAD-LEG LIFTS

Aim
To improve buttock flexibility and hip mobility. To isolate the correct 'running cycle' motion for each leg.

Area/equipment
An indoor or outdoor grid 22 yards in length. The width of the grid is variable depending on the size of the group.

Description
Player covers the length of the grid by bringing the knee of one leg quickly up to a 90-degree position. The other leg should remain as straight as possible with a very short lift away from the ground through-out the movement. The ratio should be 1 : 4, i.e. 1 lift to every 4 steps. Work one leg on the way down the grid and the other on the return.

Ball
The ball is held by the fingertips in the hand opposite to the knee performing the lift, then swapped over and held in the other hand for the return.

Key teaching points
- Do not raise knees above 90 degrees
- Strike the floor with the ball of the foot
- Keep the foot in a straight line
- Maintain correct running mechanics

What you might see	Solutions
Both knees being lifted	Player to focus on one side only. Perform the drill at a walking pace, i.e. walk, lift, walk, lift
Stuttering form and rhythm	Use marker dots to help rhythm. Work on this drill in the mechanics phase
Knee-lift angled either out or across the body	Perform drill with the arm on the knee lift side held out in a straight line with the ball in the hand. Knee to be brought up to touch the ball then returned to the ground.

Sets and reps
2 × 22 yards, 1 forwards and 1 backwards.

Variations/progressions
Vary the lift ratio, e.g. 1 : 2.

DRILL   *HIGH KNEE-LIFT SKIPS*

Aim
To improve buttock flexibility and hip mobility. To increase the range of motion (ROM) over a period of time. To develop rhythm. To increase body temperature.

Area/equipment
An indoor or outdoor grid 22 yards in length. The width of the grid is variable depending on the size of the group.

Description
Player covers the length of the grid in a high skipping motion, and returns to the start by repeating the drill backwards.

Ball
Ball to be threaded between the legs from side to side; aim to pass the ball round the back of the thigh as the knee is lifted.

Key teaching points
- Thigh to be taken past 90 degrees
- Work off the balls of the feet
- Maintain a strong core
- Maintain an upright posture
- Control the head by looking forwards at all times
- Maintain correct arm mechanics

What you might see
- Players landing on the heels

- Inconsistency of knee lift (different heights)

Solutions
- Lean forward and focus on the balls of the feet

- Knee to be raised just above waist band. Perform drill at walking pace so that the range of movement can be practised

Sets and reps
2 × 22 yards, 1 forwards and 1 backwards.

Variations/progressions
Perform the drill laterally.

DRILL   KNEE-ACROSS SKIPS

Aim
To improve outer hip flexibility and hip mobility over a period of time. To develop balance and co-ordination. To increase body temperature.

Area/equipment
An indoor or outdoor grid 22 yards in length. The width of the grid is variable depending on the size of the group.

Description
Player covers the length of the grid in a skipping motion where the knee comes across the body, and returns to the start by repeating the drill backwards.

Ball
The ball is held by the fingertips at an angle away from the body on the same side as the knee performing the outward lift. The knee is pushed out towards the ball. The ball is then swapped over and held in the other hand for the opposite knee.

Key teaching points
- Do not force an increased ROM
- Work off the balls of the feet
- Maintain a strong core
- Maintain an upright posture
- Control the head by looking forward at all times
- Use the arms primarily for balance

What you might see	Solutions
Knee-lift too high	Ball to be held below waistband
Skipping on heels	Lean slightly forwards and transfer the weight onto the balls of the feet

Sets and reps
2 × 22 yards, 1 forwards and 1 backwards.

Variations/progressions
Perform the drill laterally.

DRILL   *LATERAL RUNNING*

Aim
To develop economic knee drive, stretch the side of the quadriceps and prepare for an efficient lateral running technique. To increase body temperature.

Area/equipment
An indoor or outdoor grid 22 yards in length.

Description
Player covers the length of the grid with the left or right shoulder leading, taking short lateral steps, and returns with the opposite shoulder leading.

Ball
The ball to be transferred every three or four steps from one hand to the other.

Key teaching points
- Keep the hips square and work off the balls of the feet
- Do not skip and do not let the feet cross over
- Maintain an upright posture
- Do not sink into the hips or fold at the waist
- Do not over-stride – use short, sharp steps
- Maintain correct arm mechanics

What you might see
- Feet crossing or being brought together

- Skipping sideways

- No arm movement or arms by the sides

Solutions
- Players should focus on working with feet shoulder-width apart. The range of movement of the feet should be just outside the shoulder to just inside the shoulder

- Players to focus on stepping, not skipping, motion

- Players to hold a cricket ball in each hand, brush the side of the body with the ball and bring the ball up to the side of the face

Sets and reps
2 × 22 yards, 1 leading with the left shoulder and 1 with the right.

Variations/progressions
Practise lateral-angled zigzag runs.

DRILL PRE-TURN

Aim
To prepare the hips for a turning action without committing the whole body. To increase body temperature and improve body control.

Area/equipment
An indoor or outdoor grid 22 yards in length. The width of the grid is variable depending on the size of the group.

Description
Player covers the length of the grid by performing a lateral movement. The heel of the back foot is moved to a position almost alongside the lead foot. Just before the feet come together, the lead foot is moved away laterally. Return to the start by repeating the drill but lead with the opposite shoulder.

Ball
Ball to be held on the same side as the knee being raised. Transfer to the opposite side for the return drill.

Key teaching points
- The back foot must not cross the lead foot
- Work off the balls of the feet
- Maintain correct arm mechanics
- Maintain an upright posture
- Do not sink into the hips or fold at the waist
- Do not use a high knee-lift; the angle should be no more than 45 degrees

What you might see	Solutions
Crossing of feet	Players to focus on stepping, not skipping, motion; use marker spots to indicate where feet should be placed in pre-turn stepping
Leading leg raised	Use the arm of the leading side to press down on the thigh as a reminder that this leg remains straighter
Hips turned	Stand tall, head up, breathe in and out then hold contraction

Sets and reps
2 × 22 yards, 1 leading with left shoulder and 1 with the right.

DRILL   *CARIOCA*

Aim
To improve hip mobility and speed, which will increase the firing of nerve impulses over a period of time. To develop balance and co-ordination while moving and twisting. To increase body temperature.

Area/equipment
An indoor or outdoor grid 22 yards in length. The width of the grid is variable depending on the size of the group.

Description
Player covers the length of the grid by moving laterally. The rear foot crosses in front of the body and then moves around to the back. Simultaneously, the lead foot does the opposite. The arms also move across the front and back of the body.

Ball
Ball to be transferred from hand to hand during sideways movement.

Key teaching points
- Start slowly and build up the tempo
- Work off the balls of the feet
- Keep the shoulders square
- Do not force the ROM
- Use the arms primarily for balance

What you might see
- Torso sunk into the hips

- Co-ordination problem, i.e. unable to put other leg behind the front leg
- Arms swinging too quickly or not at all

Solutions
- Stand tall, head up, breathe in and out and hold contraction
- Practise slowly, go through the drill at walking pace

- Allow the arms to do what comes naturally. The use of the ball may prove difficult at first – initially practise without the ball

Sets and reps
2 × 22 yards, 1 leading with the left leg and 1 with the right.

Variations/progressions
Perform the drill laterally with a partner (mirror drills), i.e. one initiates or leads the movement while the other attempts to follow.

DRILL SIDE LUNGES

Aim

To stretch the inner thighs and gluteals (buttocks). To develop balance and co-ordination. To increase body temperature.

Area/equipment

An indoor or outdoor grid 22 yards in length. The width of the grid is variable depending on the size of the group.

Description

Player covers the length of the grid by performing lateral lunges. Take a wide lateral step and simultaneously lower the gluteals towards the ground. Return to the start with the opposite shoulder leading.

Ball

Transfer the ball in front of the body from hand to hand while lunging.

Key teaching points

- Do not bend at the waist or lean forwards
- Try to keep off the heels
- Maintain a strong core and keep upright
- Use the arms primarily for balance

What you might see

- Players leaning forwards

Solutions

- Keep spine in an upright, aligned position by keeping the head up and chin level

Sets and reps

2 × 22 yards, 1 leading with the left shoulder and 1 with the right.

Variations/progressions

Work in pairs facing each other and chest-passing the ball.

DRILL   *HAMSTRING BUTTOCK FLICKS*

Aim
To stretch the front and back of the thighs and improve hip mobility. To increase body temperature.

Area/equipment
An indoor or outdoor grid 22 yards in length. The width of the grid is variable depending on the size of the group.

Description
Player covers the length of the grid by moving forwards, alternating leg flicks where the heel moves up towards the buttocks. Return to the start repeating the drill backwards.

Ball
Ball to be transferred from hand to hand as quickly as possible.

Key teaching points
- Start slowly and build up the tempo
- Work off the balls of the feet
- Maintain an upright posture
- Do not sink into the hips
- Try to develop a rhythm

What you might see
- Knee raised up towards front of body

- Hands held at the back above the top of the thighs

Solutions
- Thigh to remain vertical to the ground with movement starting from below the knee. Practise the leg flick while standing still, using a wall or a partner for stability; players to look down and observe the movement required
- Encourage players to perform the drill with their hands held out in front. Remind them that during a game you do not move with their hands behind their back.

Sets and reps
2 × 22 yards, 1 forwards and 1 backwards.

Variations/progressions
- Perform the drill laterally
- Perform the drill as above but flick the heel to the outside of the buttocks.

DRILL — HEEL TO INSIDE OF THIGH SKIP

Aim
To stretch the hamstrings, groin and gluteals. To improve balance and co-ordination and to increase body temperature.

Area/equipment
An indoor or outdoor grid 22 yards in length. The width of the grid is variable depending on the size of the group.

Description
Player covers the length of the grid in a skipping motion where the heel of one leg comes up almost to touch the inside thigh of the opposite leg. Imagine there is a football on a piece of string that is hanging centrally just below your waist and you are trying to kick it with alternate heels. Return performing the movement backwards.

Ball
Ball to be transferred around the body, from left to right and right to left.

Key teaching points
- Start slowly and build up the tempo
- Work off the balls of the feet
- Maintain an upright posture
- Maintain a strong core throughout
- Use the arms for balance

What you might see
- Confusion between high-knee skip and heel to inside thigh skip

Solutions
- Heel of lifted leg to be directed towards the inside of the groin. Heel can touch the inside of the thigh as a cue for correct range of movement

Sets and reps
2 × 22 yards, 1 forwards and 1 backwards.

Variations/progressions
Perform the drill laterally.

DRILL   *SIDEWAYS HEEL FLICKS*

Aim
To stretch gluteals, outer hamstrings and outer thighs. To develop rhythm and co-ordination and to increase body temperature.

Area/equipment
An indoor or outdoor grid 22 yards in length. The width of the grid is variable depending on the size of the group.

Description
Player covers the length of the grid by performing a skipping motion where the heel is flicked up and out to the side. Complete the grid performing the drill on alternate legs before repeating backwards.

Ball
The ball to be thrown up and caught continuously.

Key teaching points
■ Start slowly and build up the tempo
■ Work off the balls of the feet
■ Maintain an upright posture and strong core
■ Use the arms for balance
■ Try to develop a rhythm

What you might see
■ Landing on flat feet and too upright

Solutions
■ Players to lean forwards slightly and transfer the weight onto the ball of the foot

Sets and reps
2 × 22 yards, 1 forwards and 1 backwards.

Variations/progressions
Alternate quickly from left shoulder to right shoulder while performing the drill.

DRILL   *HURDLE WALK*

Aim
To stretch inner and outer thighs and to increase ROM. To develop balance and co-ordination and increase body temperature.

Area/equipment
An indoor or outdoor grid 22 yards in length. The width of the grid is variable depending on the size of the group.

Description
Player covers the length of the grid by walking in a straight line and lifting alternate legs as if going over high hurdles. Return to the start repeating the drill backwards.

Ball
The ball to be transferred from side to side.

Key teaching points
- Try to keep the body square as the hips rotate
- Work off the balls of the feet
- Maintain an upright posture
- Do not sink into the hips or bend over at the waist
- Imagine that you are actually stepping over a barrier

What you might see
- The anchored foot is flat while the other leg is raised. This will cause a poor range of movement

Solutions
- Players to focus on working off the ball of the foot that is anchored. Practise by standing with feet shoulder-width apart and rising up off the heels onto the balls of the feet, holding for a second and then returning to the starting position; repeat 20–30 times. This will provide kinaesthetic feedback to the players as to what it feels like to be on the balls of the feet

Sets and reps
2 × 22 yards, 1 forwards and 1 backwards.

DRILL   *RUSSIAN WALK*

Aim
To stretch the back of the thighs. To improve hip mobility and ankle stabilisation. To develop balance and co-ordination and increase body temperature.

Area/equipment
An indoor or outdoor grid 22 yards in length. The width of the grid is variable depending on the size of the group.

Description
Player covers the length of the grid by performing a walking march with a high, extended step. Imagine that the aim is to scrape the sole/ spikes of your cricket shoe down the front of a door or a fence.

Ball
The ball to be alternated from hand to hand.

Key teaching points
- Lift the knee before extending the leg
- Work off the balls of the feet
- Try to keep off the heels, particularly on the back foot
- Keep the hips square
- Pull the toes towards the shins so that they point vertically to the sky.

What you might see
- Toe pointing out horizontally not vertically

Solutions
- Get player to pull the toe towards the shin and practise the Russian Walk on the spot before introducing walking

Sets and reps
2 × 22 yards, both forwards.

Variations/progressions
Perform the drill backwards.

DRILL   *WALKING LUNGES*

Aim
To stretch the front of the hips and thighs. To develop balance and co-ordination and increase body temperature.

Area/equipment
An indoor or outdoor grid 22 yards in length.

Description
Player covers the length of the grid by performing a walking lunge. The front leg should be bent with a 90-degree angle at the knee and the thigh in a horizontal position. The back leg should also be at a 90-degree angle but with the knee touching the ground and the thigh in a vertical position. During the lunge the player will bring both arms above the head to activate core muscles. Return to the start by repeating the drill backwards.

Ball
The ball to be held in both hands; during the lunge the ball is brought above the player's head.

Key teaching points
- Try to keep the hips square, maintain a strong core and keep upright
- Persevere with backward lunges – these are difficult to master

What you might see	Solutions
Poor balance and control	Over-striding can cause this. Ensure that players bend knee at 90-degree angle and the thigh is in the horizontal position. Use marker dots to indicate length of lunge
Stride too short causing inability to lunge properly	Focus on knee bend of 90-degree angle and keeping the thigh horizontal. Practise drill slowly on the spot

Sets and reps
2 × 22 yards, 1 forwards and 1 backwards.

Variations/progressions
- Perform the drill with handweights
- Perform the drill while catching and passing a ball in the down position
- Alternate arms above the head, one up and one down

DRILL   *WALKING HAMSTRING*

Aim

To stretch the backs of the thighs.

Area/equipment

An indoor or outdoor grid 22 yards in length. The width of the grid is variable depending on the size of the group.

Description

Player covers the length of the grid by extending the lead leg heel first on the ground, rolling onto the ball of the foot and sinking into the hips while keeping the spine straight. Walk forwards and repeat on the opposite leg. Continue in this manner, alternating the lead leg. For comfort, cross the arms.

Ball

Alternate the ball from side to side.

Key teaching points

- Keep the spine straight
- Do not bend over
- Control the head by looking forwards at all times
- Work at a steady pace, do not rush

What you might see	Solutions
Head down, leaning forward	Players to keep chin up and focus on something horizontally in line with the eyes
Bent at the waist	Hips to be kept square; trunk and spine must remain in an upright position

Sets and reps

2 × 22 yards, 1 forwards and 1 backwards.

Variations/progressions

Perform drill laterally.

DRILL

WALL DRILL – LEG OUT AND ACROSS BODY

Aim
To increase the ROM in the hip region. To increase body temperature.

Area/equipment
A wall or fence to lean against.

Description
Player faces and leans against the wall/fence at a 20–30-degree angle, and swings the leg across the body from one side to the other. Repeat on the other leg.

Key teaching points
- Do not force an increased ROM
- Work off the ball of the support foot
- Lean with both hands against the wall/fence
- Keep the hips square
- Do not look down
- Gradually speed up the movement

What you might see
- No heel raise off the ground

Solutions
- Players should focus on leaning forwards and transferring weight onto the ball of the foot while the leg is swung across the body. Place a cricket bail under the heel of the planted foot

Sets and reps
7–20 on each leg.

Variations/progressions
Lean against a partner.

DRILL

WALL DRILL –
LINEAR LEG FORWARD/BACK

Aim
To increase the ROM in the hip region. To increase body temperature.

Area/equipment
A wall or fence to lean against.

Description
Player stands side-on to the wall/fence and, supporting himself with the arm closest to the wall, takes the opposite leg back and swings it forward in a straight line. Repeat with the other leg.

Key teaching points
- Do not force an increased ROM
- Work off the ball of the support foot
- Do not look down
- Gradually increase speed

What you might see
- No heel raise off the ground

Solutions
- Players should focus on leaning forwards and transferring weight onto the ball of the foot while the leg is swung across the body. Place a cricket bail under the heel of the planted foot

Sets and reps
7–15 on each leg.

Variations/progressions
Lean against a partner.

DRILL

WALL DRILL –
KNEE ACROSS BODY

Aim
To increase the ROM in the hip region. To increase body temperature.

Area/equipment
A wall or fence to lean against.

Description
Player faces and leans against the wall/fence at an angle of 20–30 degrees, and, from a standing position, drives one knee upwards and across the body. Repeat with the other leg.

Key teaching points
- Do not force an increased ROM
- Work off the ball of the support foot
- Lean with both hands against the wall/fence
- Keep the hips square
- Do not look down
- Gradually increase speed
- Imagine you are trying to get your knee up and across your body to the opposite hip

What you might see
- No heel raise off the ground

Solutions
- Players should focus on leaning forwards and transferring weight onto the ball of the foot while the leg is swung across the body. Place a cricket bail under the heel of the planted foot

Sets and reps
7–20 on each leg.

Variations/progressions
Lean against a partner.

DRILL   *SELECTION OF SPRINTS*

Aim
To increase the intensity of the warm-up and prepare players for maximum exertion. To speed up the firing rate of neuromuscular messages. To increase body temperature.

Area/equipment
An indoor or outdoor grid 22 yards in length. The width of the grid is variable depending on the size of the group. Sprint one way only, perform a jog-back recovery on the outside of the grid.

Description
Player to start from different angles – e.g. side-on, backwards, etc. – and to accelerate into a forward running motion down the grid.

Ball
The ball can be used to run onto field, turn and throw etc. during the sprint. This makes the sprinting very cricket-specific.

Key teaching points
- Maintain good running mechanics
- Ensure that players alternate the lead foot

Sets and reps
1 set of 5 sprints, varying the start position.

Variations/progressions
- Include swerving sprints
- Include turns in the sprints

DRILL   *GRID VARIATIONS*

Sidestep back grid

Aim
To stimulate and motivate players with a variety of movement patterns.

Area/equipment
Mark out an indoor or outdoor grid 22 yards in length with markers placed at 5-yard intervals. The width of the grid is variable depending on the size of the group. Place a line of markers on each side of the grid about 2 yards away with 1 yard between each marker.

Description
Perform Dynamic Flex down the grid with the group splitting around the end markers to return on the outside of the grid. On reaching the side markers the player should zigzag back through them.

Ball
The ball is held in one hand as the arm is rotated, then swapped over and held in the other hand for the return.

Key teaching points
The timing is crucial – players should be constantly on the move.

Sets and reps
Player can perform the entire Dynamic Flex warm-up in this manner.

Variations/progressions
Replace the markers on the outside of the grid with Fast Foot Ladders or hurdles.

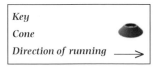

Key
Cone
Direction of running

Figure 1.2 Sidestep back grid

GRID VARIATIONS cont.

Split grid

Aim
To improve ball control and passing skills.

Area/equipment
Mark out an indoor or outdoor grid 22 yards in length with an additional 10 yards on the end (use different coloured markers). The width of the grid is variable depending on the size of the group. Place a ball between the two grids for each player who will have just completed his/her Dynamic Flex drill.

Description
Perform Dynamic Flex down the grid over the first 22 yards and on reaching the additional 10-yard area, perform ball skills up and back over it. On completing the ball skills, pass the ball to the player coming on, who will have just completed his/her Dynamic Flex drill.

Key	
Cone	
Direction of running	→

Ball
The ball is held in one hand as the player goes up the channel, then swapped over and held in the other hand for the return.

Key teaching points
■ The timing is crucial – players should be constantly on the move
■ Players should communicate with one another, e.g. when passing the ball

Sets and reps
Player can perform the entire Dynamic Flex warm-up in this manner.

Variations/progressions
Vary the ball skill drills.

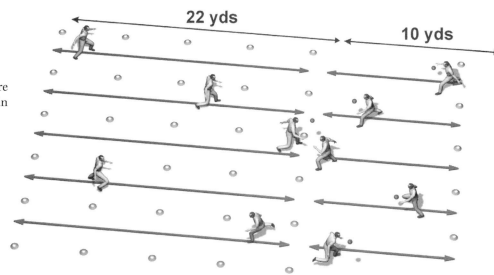

Figure 1.3 Split grid

GRID VARIATIONS cont.

Circle grid

Aim
To stimulate and motivate players, improve and challenge Dynamic Flex movements while moving around a circle.

Area/equipment
Mark out an indoor or outdoor grid with a circle of markers 20 yards in diameter and a centre circle of markers 5 yards in diameter. The diameter of the circle is variable depending on the size of the group.

Description
Perform Dynamic Flex around the outside of the circle changing directions, forwards and backwards. Then for certain drills players should move inwards and outwards to the centre circle, i.e. hamstring walk.

Key teaching points
Timing and change of direction is very important.

Sets and reps
Players can perform the entire Dynamic Flex Warm-up in this manner.

Variations/progressions
Introduce the ball.

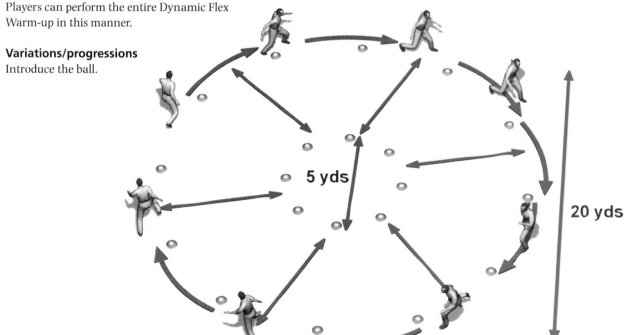

5 yds

20 yds

Figure 1.4 Circle grid

CHAPTER 2 RUNNING FORM FOR CRICKET

THE MECHANICS OF MOVEMENT

There is a great deal of multi-directional movement that includes running used in the playing of cricket. Many years ago future cricketers would develop a lot of their skills playing in the streets, on school parks and in PE lessons. Incredibly, in the past 25–30 years, more than 70 per cent of children fail to participate in any sport on leaving school. In some primary schools children are lucky to get 12 hours physical activity a year. Moreover, governing bodies continue to sell off playgrounds and playing fields for housing developments, leaving children and teenagers with nowhere to practise sports. There-fore, one of the most damaging assumptions made by coaches is that players have been taught to run correctly within the education system or that running is something that occurs naturally. One will always encounter naturally gifted players who are explosive and who make fast running, jumping and sidestepping look easy (although these are few and far between). For a coach to neglect running and movement mechanics in cricket training is to ignore the potential in many players.

How often one hears comments in the game of cricket such as, 'If I'd only moved faster I would have made the catch!' or 'Good technical skills, but too slow'. Many young players lack the balance, co-ordination, visual awareness and running and movement skills to react to the speed of the game. All players, whatever their age, can improve speed, acceleration and general movement skills by practising and applying the correct mechanics.

The best players and teams in the world are able to control the pace of their play effectively and economically. They have the ability to put pressure on the opposition by being quicker between the wickets, faster and more accurate in the outfield and generally reacting more explosively than the opposition.

The game of cricket can be described as an explosive, multi-directional, interval activity. The bouts of activity vary according to type of bowlers, time between each ball bowled, runs scored and time between each over. Therefore, training and con-ditioning programmes should attempt to mirror the specific demands of the actual game.

Arm mechanics

There is no need to focus on techniques for the 100 m sprint. Cricket players very rarely have the space to plane out after 30 m or relax and think about 'jelly jaw' exercises. Cricket requires a sound basic technique and, the ability to change from correct running mechanics to bending and scooping the ball off the ground, throwing it back to the wicketkeeper while on the move, then returning to reassert good mechanics to decelerate or change direction.

Remember that many coaches and managers are first and foremost looking for the players who are explosive over the first 5 yards. Using the correct arm drive will go a long way to assisting players of all shapes and sizes to be quicker in this area.

Running form
ARMS
- Elbows should be held at 90 degrees
- Hands and shoulders should be relaxed
- The insides of the wrists should brush against the hips
- The hands should move from the buttock cheeks to the chest or head

Lift mechanics

Coaching players to get their knees up high, particularly in the first few yards of the acceleration phase, only makes them slower. Using high knee-lift during the acceleration phase has the negative effect of minimizing force development, therefore not enough power is produced to propel the body forwards in an explosive action. During the first few yards of acceleration, short, sharp steps are required. These steps generate a high degree of force, which takes the body from a stationary position into the first controlled explosive steps.

Cricket is a multi-sprint stop-and-start sport, so the first phases of acceleration and re-acceleration are crucial. Look and listen for the following in a player's initial acceleration strides:

- 45-degree knee-lift

- Foot-to-floor contact with the ball of the foot

- Front of the foot staying in a linear position

- Knees coming up in a vertical line

- Foot-to-floor contact making a tapping noise, not a thud or slap

- The foot and knee should not splay in or out, or power will not be transferred correctly

- Keeping off the heels

- On the lift, the foot will transfer from pointing slightly down to pointing slightly up

Posture

Posture is a crucial part of all movements required for cricket including sprinting, jumping and turning. The spine should be kept as straight as possible at all times. This means that a player who has jumped for the ball now has to run into space, and needs to transfer to the correct running form as quickly as possible. Running with a straight spine does not mean running bolt upright; one can keep the spine straight using a slight lean forwards. What *is* to be avoided is players running while sinking into their hips – which looks like being folded up in the middle – or sinking too deep when landing after jumping, because this prevents instant effective transfer of power.

Core control is another important factor in developing and utilising a strong posture. Core development and maintenance for cricket players is very important and will be touched on briefly later in this book. A simple rule prior to and throughout the performing of all the drills in this book is as follows: engage your core muscles by simply breathing in, breathing out and then breathing in again, then try to maintain this feeling throughout the exercise – not forgetting to breathe normally! This will help prevent your pelvic wall from moving around, which causes a loss of power, and will also protect the lower back, hamstrings and girdle area from injury.

Mechanics for deceleration

The ability of a cricket player to stop quickly, change direction and accelerate away from scooping the ball off the ground is key to building successful teams. You can practise this: do not leave it to chance, include it in your sessions

- *Posture* – lean back. This alters the angle of the spine and hips, which control foot placement. Foot contact with the ground will now transfer to the heel, which acts like a brake.

- *Fire the arms* – by firing the arms quickly, the energy produced will increase the frequency of heel contact to the ground. Think of it like pressing harder on the brakes in a car.

The running techniques described in this chapter cover basic mechanics for cricket-specific techniques where running, jumping and turning are all important parts of the game and are developed through the use of hurdles, stride frequency canes and running technique drills.

Mechanics for change of direction, including lateral and turning movements

LATERAL SIDESTEP

Do not use a wide stance as this will decrease the potential for power generation as you attempt to push off/away. Do not pull with the leading foot but rather push off the back foot. Imagine that your car has broken down and that you need to move it to a service station – would you pull it? No, you would push it. Ensure that a strong arm drive is used at all times but particularly during the push-off phase.

MAKING A 180-DEGREE TURN – THE DROP STEP

Most players use too many movements to make a 180-degree turn. Many jump up on the spot first, then take 3 or 4 steps to make the turn, others will jump up and perform the turn in the air with a complete lack of control. When practised, the drop step turn looks seamless and is far quicker.

For a right-shoulder turn the player starts by opening up the right groin and simultaneously transferring the weight onto the left foot. The right foot is raised slightly off the ground and, using a swinging action, is moved around to the right to face the opposite direction. The right foot is planted and the player drives/pushes off the left foot, remembering to use a strong arm drive. Do not overstretch on the turn. Players may find it helpful initially to tell themselves to 'turn and go'. With practice players will develop an efficient and economic seamless turn.

Movement checklists for players

The movement checklists for players will help coaches and trainers identify the correct and incorrect form for multi-directional movement. It also provides solutions that can be simply implemented to rectify problems. These solutions can be used with the very young, youth and senior players. If you are ever in doubt regarding a player's movement you must consult a physiotherapist or doctor to ensure that there is not a physiological problem that may require medical intervention.

The movement checklists can be used in all areas of the SAQ Continuum including explosion when resistance equipment is being used. The golden rule is that correct mechanics and form always comes first.

RUNNING – STARTING POSITION

Correct	Incorrect	Solution
FEET POSITION ■ Shoulder-width apart ■ On the ball of the foot ■ In a straight line	■ Too wide ■ Too close ■ On the toes ■ On the heels ■ Weight outside or inside ■ Pointing in ■ Splayed out	■ Use chalk marks or marker spots on the ground to indicate best position ■ Lean slightly forwards on the ball of the foot ■ Position feet in a straight line ■ Keep heels off the ground ■ Use straight lines on the ground to position feet ■ Use chalk to mark around the foot on hard surfaces so player can stand in the outline to ensure correct positioning
ARMS ■ Held ready with 90-degree angle at the elbow ■ One forward, one back ■ Relaxed	■ Arms by the side ■ Shoulders shrugged with arms too high ■ Tight and restricted	■ Provide constant feedback on arm technique ■ Practise holding arms in correct position, then accelerate arms as if starting to run – perform Partner arm drive drill (see drills, below) ■ Use string looped between index finger and thumb and point of elbow to hold correct position of 90 degrees
HIPS ■ Need to be high or tall and slightly forwards	■ Sunk ■ Twisted	■ Hold head tall and upright ■ Hold stomach in, focus on keeping the hips high and lean slightly forwards in the running direction ■ Keep chin off chest ■ Focus on a good linear body position
HEAD POSITION ■ Held high ■ Eyes forward	■ Held down, turned ■ Looking up	■ Imagine you are looking over a fence that comes up to your nose ■ Pick an object in the distance and focus on it

RUNNING – ACCELERATION PHASE

Correct	Incorrect	Solution
HAND ■ Fingertips gently touching thumb tip	■ Soft (most common) ■ Droopy ■ Tightly closed	■ Hold post-it note or something similar between index finger and thumb
ARM ACTION ■ Fast ■ 90-degree angle at elbow ■ One forward, one back behind hips	■ Slow to medium	■ Perform Partner arm drive drills (see drills below) ■ Use short, sharp sets of on-the-spot fast arm bursts ■ Use light handweights for 8–9 seconds then perform contrast arm drives as quickly as possible afterwards
ARM DRIVE ■ Chin to waist ■ Wrist or hand firm	■ Arms across body ■ Forearm chop ■ At the side ■ Held in stiff, angled position	■ Perform Partner arm drive drills (see drills below) ■ Brush the inside of the wrist against waistband, then raise thumb to touch chin ■ Use long elastic bands looped between index finger and thumb and elbow, then perform arm drives ■ Perform arm drive drill in front of mirror for feedback ■ Perform Buttock bounces (see drills, below)
HEAD ■ Held high ■ Keep up ■ Eyes forward	■ Held down ■ Turned ■ Looking up ■ Rocking from side to side	■ Imagine you are looking over a fence that comes up to your nose ■ Pick an object in the distance and focus on it
BODY POSITION – TRUNK ■ Tall ■ Strong	■ Sunk ■ Soft ■ Bent	■ Head up; hold stomach in, hips high, slightly forward and square
FOOT ACTION ■ Active ■ Plantar flex (toe down) ■ Dorsiflex (toe up) down)/dorsiflex (toe up)	■ Flat ■ Heel first to touch ground ■ Inactive plantar flex (toe	■ Focus on the balls of the feet ■ Remove built-up heeled shoes ■ Practise plantar/dorsiflex skip ■ Ensure there is a slight fowards body lean ■ Keep head up; do not sink into the hips

RUNNING – ACCELERATION PHASE (continued)

Correct	Incorrect	Solution
HEELS ■ Raised	■ Down, contacting ground ■ Heels first to touch ground	■ Focus on the balls of the feet ■ Remove built-up heeled shoes ■ Roll up cloth or paper, hold with tape into a small ball, slightly larger than a marble. Place one in each shoe, under heels
HIPS ■ Tall ■ Square ■ Up/forward ■ Firm ■ Still	■ Bent ■ Sunk ■ Turned	■ Hold head tall and upright ■ Hold stomach in, focus on keeping the hips square to the running direction ■ Practise Buttock bounces (see drills, below)
KNEES ■ Linear ■ Below waist ■ Foot just off ground ■ Drive forward	■ Across body ■ Splayed ■ Too high with foot too high off ground	■ Practise Dead-leg run (see drills, below) ■ Teacher/coach to place hands where knees should lift to, practise bringing the knees up to the hands while running on the spot ■ Use coloured tape, attach from above to below the knee in a straight line, either on skin or clothing. The tape should now go across the centre of the kneecap. Now perform on-the-spot running drills in front of a mirror, focusing on keeping the coloured tape in a straight line
RELAXATION ■ Relaxed ■ Calm ■ Comfortable	■ Tense ■ Too loose ■ Distracted	■ Imagine accelerating quickly with power and grace, but staying calm and relaxed ■ Breathing to be controlled

RUNNING – AFTER ACCELERATION (PLANING-OUT PHASE)

Correct	Incorrect	Solution
STRIDE LENGTH ■ Medium for individual	■ Too long ■ Too short ■ Erratic	■ Use marker spots or stride frequency canes to mark out correct distances of stride length
STRIDE FREQUENCY ■ Balanced for individual	■ Too quick ■ Too slow	■ Use marker spots or stride frequency canes to mark out correct distances of stride length so that frequency can be determined
ARM ACTION ■ Fast ■ 90-degree angle at elbow ■ Hands above shoulders, behind hips	■ Slow to medium	■ Perform Partner arm drive drills (see drills below) ■ Use short, sharp sets of on-the-spot fast arm bursts ■ Use light handweights for 8–9 seconds then perform contrast arm drives as quickly as possible afterwards
ARM DRIVE ■ Chin to waist	■ Arms across body ■ Forearms chopping ■ Arms at the side ■ Arms held in stiff angled position	■ Perform Partner arm drive drills (see drills, below) ■ Brush the inside of the wrist against waistband, then thumb rises to touch chin ■ Place long elastic bands between index finger and thumb and looped around elbow, then perform arm drives ■ Perform arm drive drill in front of a mirror for feedback ■ Perform Buttock bounces (see drills, below)
HEAD ■ Held high ■ Keep up ■ Eyes forward	■ Held down ■ Turned ■ Looking up ■ Rocking from side to side	■ Imagine you are looking over a fence that comes up to your nose ■ Pick an object in the distance and focus on it
BODY POSITION – TRUNK ■ Tall	■ Sunk ■ Soft ■ Bent	■ Head up; hold stomach in, hips high, slightly forward and square

RUNNING – AFTER ACCELERATION (PLANING-OUT PHASE) (continued)

Correct	Incorrect	Solution
FOOT ACTION ■ Active ■ Plantar flex (toe down) ■ Dorsiflex (toe up)	■ Flat ■ Heel first to touch ground ■ Inactive plantar flex (toe down)/dorsiflex (toe up)	■ Focus on the balls of the feet ■ Remove built-up heeled shoes ■ Practise plantar/dorsiflex skip ■ Ensure there is a slight fowards body lean ■ Keep head up; do not sink into the hips
RELAXATION ■ Relaxed ■ Calm ■ Comfortable	■ Tense ■ Too loose ■ Distracted	■ Imagine accelerating quickly with power and grace, but remaining calm and relaxed ■ Breathing to be controlled

LATERAL STEPPING

Correct	Incorrect	Solution
FOOT ACTION ■ Work off the ball of the foot	■ On the heels ■ Flat-footed	■ Lean slightly fowards even when stepping sideways ■ Provide constant feedback to keep off heels ■ Keep hips tall and strong; this helps control power and prevent flat-footed weight transfer
■ Feet shoulder-width apart	■ Too wide ■ Too close ■ Crossed ■ Pointing in ■ Splayed out	■ Use marker spots to indicate best foot position for lateral stepping ■ Practise stepping slowly at first, then build up speed gradually
■ Drive off trailing foot	■ Reach with leading foot ■ Flat-footed ■ On heels ■ Feet pointing in or splayed	■ Use marker spots to indicate best foot positions ■ Use coloured tape, attach from tongue to end of shoes in straight line; work in front of mirror, focusing on keeping the lines on the foot straight ■ Tape a ball of paper under the heel of each foot ■ Use angled boards to step off
HIPS ■ Firm ■ Controlled ■ Square ■ High	■ Soft ■ Twisted ■ Angled ■ Leaning too far forwards ■ Bent at the waist ■ Sunk	■ Hold head tall ■ Hold stomach in ■ Focus on keeping hips square
ARMS ■ 90-degree arm drive ■ Fast and strong drive	■ Arm across the body ■ No arm drive at all ■ Arms too tight and restricted ■ Arms moving forwards but not driving backwards behind the hips	■ Perform Partner arm drive drills (see drills below), practise moving sideways ■ Perform Mirror drills (see drills, below) ■ Constant positive feedback
TRUNK ■ Strong and firm ■ Slight lean forward	■ Too upright ■ Leaning too far forwards ■ Bent at the waist ■ Leaning back	■ Perform Mirror drills (see drills, below) ■ Keep head looking forward and still ■ Hold stomach in ■ Slight knee bend only

LATERAL TURNING – 90 DEGREES

Correct	Incorrect	Solution
FEET ■ Shoulder-width apart	■ Together ■ Too wide ■ Crossed	■ Use chalk marks or marker spots to indicate best starting and finishing position
ON THE TURN ■ Feet stay shoulder-width apart ■ Work on the balls of the feet	■ Come together ■ Cross ■ Go apart too wide ■ Go onto heels ■ Go onto toes	■ Use chalk marks or marker spots to indicate best starting and finishing posiion ■ Practise single turn in front of a mirror
FOOT DRIVE ■ Drive off trailing foot	■ Forward reach ■ Jump on the spot ■ Rock back on heels	■ Keep trunk firm ■ Get players to say the words 'push' on the drive and 'off' on the turn, either in their heads or out loud ■ Practise lateral sidesteps slowly then build up speed ■ Maintain good arm drive
HIPS ■ High, slightly forwards and square ■ Hip before knee	■ Hips low and sunk ■ Angled not square ■ Trunk leaning too far forwards or too upright	■ Keep hips firm, tall and leaning forwards ■ Use arm drive with hips to assist turn ■ Keep hips square when turning ■ Practise turns slowly at first
HEAD ■ Keep up ■ Off the chest ■ Eyes looking forward ■ Head and hip work simultaneously during turn	■ Floppy ■ Down ■ Angled ■ Back	■ Pick two distant objects, one in front of you, the other in the direction you are turning to. Initially focus on the object in front, then on the turn refocus on the second object

TURN – 180 DEGREES

Correct	Incorrect	Solution
INITIAL MOVEMENT ■ Seamless ■ Movement smooth, no punctuations ■ Sequence is drop, step and go (1–2–3)	■ Jump up ■ Step back ■ Twist	■ Practise drop step, the opening of the leg to point in the direction of the turn; the trailing foot then pushes off ■ Practise saying out loud, 'drop, step and go' ■ Practise slowly at first, gradually developing speed ■ Practise facing a wall, so when you turn the back step is prevented ■ Practise turn in front of a mirror ■ Use video of turn
FEET ■ Shoulder-width apart	■ Together ■ Too wide ■ Crossed	■ Use chalk marks or marker spots to indicate best starting and finishing position
ARM DRIVE ■ 90-degree arm drive same as for lateral ■ Fast and strong drive	■ Arm across the body ■ No arm drive at all ■ Arms too tight and restricted ■ Arms moving forward but not driving backwards behind the hips	■ Perform Partner arm drive drills (see drills below) and practise moving sideways ■ Perform mirror drills (see drills below) ■ Provide constant positive feedback
HEAD ■ Up ■ Eyes looking forward	■ Down ■ Angled ■ Turned	■ Pick two distant objects, one in front of you, the other behind. Initially focus on the object in front, then on the turn refocus on the second object
HIPS ■ High, slightly forwards and square ■ Hip before knee	■ Hip low and sunk ■ Angled not square ■ Trunk leaning too far forward or too upright	■ Keep hips firm, tall and leaning forwards ■ Use arm drive with hips to assist turn ■ Keep hips square when turning ■ Practise turns slowly at first

JUMPING

Correct	Incorrect	Solution
ARM DRIVE ■ Arms at 90-degree angle at the elbow, working together, from behind the hips to above the head	■ No arm movement ■ Arms not working together ■ Only one arm used	■ Practise with a balloon. Hold the balloon in front, below the chest, with both hands, and then throw it over the back of the head ■ Once the ballon drill is perfected introduce the throwing of the ballon with a jump ■ Demonstrate the difference between jumping with and without arm drive. Attempt a jump with arms at the side then repeat with positive arm action
PRE-JUMP HIPS ■ Tall, slightly forwards	■ Bent ■ Sunk (most common)	■ Keep hips firm, tall and leaning forwards ■ Keep hips square when jumping ■ Hold head up and stomach in
TAKE-OFF FEET ■ On the balls of the feet	■ Flat-footed ■ On the heels ■ On the toes	■ Provide constant feedback to keep off heels ■ Keep hips tall and strong; this helps control power and prevent flat-footed weight transfer ■ Use a small round stick or old books half an inch thick. Place under both heels so that weight is forced onto the ball of the foot. Practise jumping in this position
LANDING ■ On the balls of the feet ■ Weight equally balanced on both feet when possible	■ On the toes ■ Heels ■ Unbalanced	■ Practise multiple bunny hops, landing on the balls of the feet, so that correct foot-to-ground contact is practised ■ Tape a ball of paper (size of a marble) under the heel of each foot ■ Draw small circles or use small marker spots (2–3 inches in diameter) as landing markers for the balls of the feet
TRUNK ■ Tall, hips leaning slightly forwards ■ Firm and relaxed	■ Sunk ■ Bent at the waist ■ Twisted ■ Uncontrolled	■ Breathe in and hold stomach firm; keep head high

JUMPING (continued)

Correct	Incorrect	Solution
HIPS ■ Firm ■ Tall ■ Leaning slightly forwards	■ Hips low and sunk ■ Angled, not square ■ Trunk leaning too far forwards or too upright	■ Keep hips firm, tall and leaning forwards ■ Use arm drive with hips to assist control ■ Keep hips square when landing ■ Practise landing by simply jumping off a step or small box ■ Imagine perfect body position

DECELERATION

Correct	Incorrect	Solution
ARMS ■ Angled 90 degrees at elbow ■ Decrease speed of drive on deceleration	■ Slow arm drive ■ No arm drive ■ Arms dropped by the sides	■ Provide feedback of 'drive arms' as soon as deceleration commences ■ Use string or elastic bands looped around index finger and thumb and point of elbow to hold correct position of 90 degrees ■ Use light handweights that are released on the deceleration phase
FEET ■ Shorten stride to smaller steps	■ Maintain long strides	■ Use coloured canes, marker dots or a short piece of outdoor Fast Food Ladder on the deceleration phase
HEAD ■ Slightly raised above horizontal plane ■ Eyes up	■ Chin down on chest ■ Head turned to one side	■ Prior to deceleration phase pick an object in the distance that is slightly higher than the horizon, thus requiring the head to be lifted ■ Coach to call 'head up' as deceleration phase begins
HIPS ■ Leaning back	■ Remaining forward ■ Lopsided ■ Sunk	■ Focus on the head being brought up; this will change the angle of the hips
TRUNK ■ Brought upright	■ Remaining tilted forwards ■ Bent	■ Get player to focus on: 1. Head up 2. Trunk up 3. Hips back Work on this combination during deceleration
HEEL ■ Weight transferred to heel ■ Heel first	■ On the toes ■ Too much weight forward on the balls of the feet	■ Get athlete to focus on: 1. Head up 2. Trunk up 3. Hips back Work on this combination during deceleration. This will also impact on the spine and transfer to the heel coming down to the ground *first* for deceleration

DRILL ARM MECHANICS – PARTNER DRILLS

Aim
To perfect the correct arm technique for running in cricket.

Area/equipment
The player works with a partner.

Description
Players stand with their partner behind them. The partner holds the palms of his/her hands in line with the player's elbows, fingers pointing upwards. Players fire the arms as if sprinting so that the elbows smack into their partner's palms.

Key teaching points
- Arms should not move across the body
- Elbows should be at 90 degrees
- Hands and shoulders should be relaxed
- The insides of the wrists should brush against the hips
- ROM – the hands should move from the buttock cheeks to the chest or head
- Encourage speed of movement to hear the smack

Sets and reps
3 sets of 16 reps, with 1 minute recovery between each set.

Variations/progressions
Use light handweights for the first 2 sets; perform the last set without.

DRILL ARM MECHANICS – MIRROR DRILLS

Aim
To perfect the correct arm technique for running in cricket.

Area/equipment
A large mirror.

Description
Players stand in front of the mirror with arms ready for sprinting and perform short bursts of arm drives. The mirror is used as a feedback tool to perfect the technique.

Key teaching points
- Arms should not move across the body
- Elbows should be at 90 degrees
- Hands and shoulders should be relaxed
- The insides of the wrists should brush against the hips
- Ensure that the player performs a full ROM – the hands should move from the buttock cheeks to the chest or head

Sets and reps
3 sets of 16 reps with 1 minute recovery between each set.

Variations/progressions
Use light handweights for the first 2 sets; perform the last set without.

DRILL **ARM MECHANICS – BUTTOCK BOUNCES**

Aim
To develop explosive arm drive.

Area/equipment
Suitable ground surface.

Description
Players sit on the floor with their legs straight out in front of them and fire their arms rapidly in short bursts. The power generated should be great enough to raise the buttocks off the floor in a bouncing manner.

Key teaching points
- Arms should not move across the body
- Elbows should be at 90 degrees
- Hands and shoulders should be relaxed
- The insides of the wrists should brush against the hips
- ROM – the hands should move from the buttock cheeks to the chest or head
- Encourage speed of movement to hear the smack

Sets and reps
3 sets of 6 reps; each rep is 6–8 explosive arm drives with 1 minute recovery between each set.

Variations/progressions
Use light handweights for the first 2 sets; perform the last set without.

DRILL *RUNNING FORM – LEADING LEG RUN*

Aim
To develop quick, efficient steps and running techniques.

Area/equipment
Indoor or outdoor area. Using hurdles, markers or sticks, place approximately 8 obstacles in a straight line at 2-foot intervals. Place a marker 1 yard from each end of the line to mark a start and finish.

Description
Players run down the line of obstacles, crossing over each one with the same leading leg. The aim is to just clear the obstacles. Repeat the drill using the opposite leg as the lead.

Key teaching points
- The knee-lift should be no more than 45 degrees
- Use short, sharp steps
- Maintain strong arm mechanics
- Maintain an upright posture
- Stand tall and do not sink into the hips

Sets and reps
1 set of 6 reps, 3 leading with the left leg and 3 with the right.

Variations/progressions
- A good drill for changing direction after running in a straight line is to place 3 markers at the end of the obstacles at different angles 2–3 yards away; on leaving the last obstacle, the player sprints out to the marker nominated by the coach
- Vary the distance between the hurdles to achieve different stride lengths
- Batsmen to run with a bat in their hand; also, later in the season, players should attempt drills in cricket pads and helmet
- Bowlers perform drill with ball in hand

Key	
Direction of running	→
Cone	●
Hurdle	⌒
Left foot	◖●
Right foot	◖○

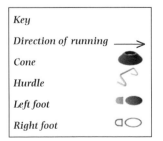

Figure 2.3 Leading leg run

DRILL — RUNNING FORM – QUICK SIDESTEP DEVELOPMENT

Aim
To develop correct, precise and controlled lateral stepping movements.

Area/equipment
Indoor or outdoor area. Place 3 hurdles side by side about 18 inches apart.

Description
Players stand on the outside of either hurdle 1 or hurdle 3 so that they will step over the middle of each hurdle. Players perform lateral movement mechanics while clearing each hurdle. On clearing hurdle 3, repeat the drill in the opposite direction.

Key teaching points
- Maintain correct lateral running form/mechanics
- Maintain correct arm mechanics
- Do not sink into the hips
- Keep the head up
- Do not lean too far forwards
- Use small steps and work off the balls of the feet
- Do not use an excessively high knee-lift

Sets and reps
2 sets of 10 reps, 5 to the left and 5 to the right with a 60-second recovery between sets.

Variations/progressions
- Work with a coach, who should randomly direct the player over the hurdles
- Add 2 Macro V Hurdles to add lift variations
- Work in groups of 3; Player 1 works through the hurdles, Players 2 and 3 stand at either end, and throw and catch the ball as Player 1 reaches their end (see Fig. 2.4(a))
- Player 1 can also turn after stepping over the last hurdle, and receive the ball from a player (see Fig. 2.4(b))

Figure 2.4(a) Quick sidestep

Key
Direction of running →
Cone
Hurdle

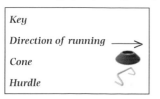
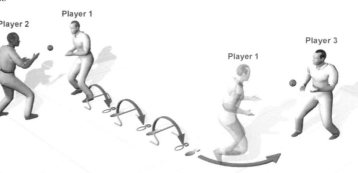

Figure 2.4(b) Quick sidestep

DRILL

RUNNING FORM –
LATERAL FIELDING DEVELOPMENT

Aim
To develop efficient and economical lateral sidesteps while catching and throwing the ball.

Area/equipment
Indoor or outdoor area. Place 8 Micro V Hurdles side on, 1 yard apart and staggered laterally. Position a finish marker in the same pattern as the hurdles.

Description
Player 1 works inside the channel created by the hurdles and steps over each hurdle with one foot as he moves laterally down and across the channel. On stepping over the outside hurdle a ball is thrown to him to catch and return by Player 2 situated on that side. This action is also repeated on the opposite side with Player 3. After receiving the ball Player 2 and 3 walk backwards into position ready for the next time Player 1 steps over the outside hurdle.

Key teaching points
- Bring the knee up to 45degrees over the hurdle
- Do not 'overstride' across the hurdle
- Maintain correct arm mechanics and a strong arm drive
- Keep the hips square
- Do not sink into the hips

Sets and reps
2 sets of 3 reps with a walk-back recovery between reps and 2 minutes between sets.

Variations/progressions
Perform the drill backwards.

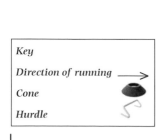

Key

Direction of running ——→

Cone

Hurdle

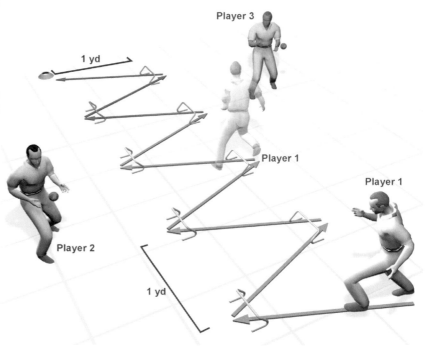

Figure 2.5 Lateral fielding development

DRILL

RUNNING FORM –
LATERAL STEPS

Aim
To develop efficient and economical lateral steps.

Area/equipment
Indoor or outdoor area. Using hurdles, markers or sticks, place approximately 8 obstacles in a straight line at 2-foot intervals. Place a marker 1 yard from each end of the line to mark a start and finish.

Description
Players step over each obstacle while moving sideways.

Key teaching points
- Bring the knee up to just below 45 degrees
- Do not skip sideways – step!
- Push off from the back foot
- Do not pull with the lead foot
- Maintain correct arm mechanics
- Maintain an upright posture
- Keep the hips square
- Do not sink into the hips

Sets and reps
1 set of 6 reps, 3 leading with the left shoulder and 3 with the right.

Variations/progressions
- Use light handweights – accelerate off the end of the last obstacle and drop the handweights during this phase
- Place several different-coloured markers 2 yards from the last hurdle at different angles; as the player leaves the last hurdle the coach nominates a marker for the player to accelerate to and either catch or field a ball thrown to them by the coach
- Players to hold a ball in their hand while performing the drill

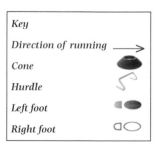

Key

Direction of running	→
Cone	
Hurdle	
Left foot	
Right foot	

Figure 2.6 Lateral steps

DRILL   *RUNNING FORM – 1-2-3 LIFT*

Aim
To develop an efficient leg cycle, rhythm, power and foot placement.

Area/equipment
Indoor or outdoor area 30–40 yards long.

Description
Players move in a straight line and after every third step the leg is brought up in an explosive action to 90 degrees. Continue the drill over the length prescribed working the same leg, and then repeat the drill leading with the other leg.

Key teaching points
- Keep the hips square
- Work off the balls of the feet
- Try to develop and maintain a rhythm
- Keep eyes and head up and look ahead
- Maintain correct arm mechanics
- Maintain an upright posture
- Leg to be snapped quickly up and down

Sets and reps
1 set of 6 reps, 3 leading with the left leg and 3 with the right.

Variations/progressions
- Alternate the lead leg during a repetition
- Vary the lift sequence, e.g. 1-2-3-4-lift, etc.
- Perform the drill with the ball in hand

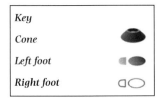

Key	
Cone	
Left foot	
Right foot	

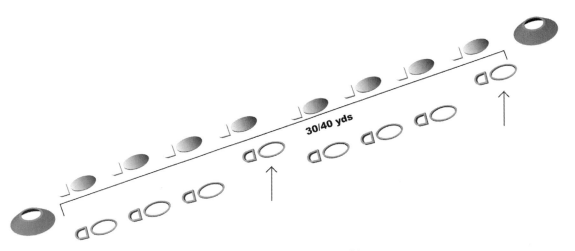

30/40 yds

Figure 2.7 1-2-3 lift

DRILL   *JUMPING – SINGLE JUMPS*

Aim
To develop jumping techniques, power, speed and control.

Area/equipment
Indoor or outdoor area. Ensure the surface is clear of any obstacles. Use 7- or 12-inch hurdles.

Description
Players jump over a single hurdle and on landing walk back to the start point to repeat the drill.

Key teaching points
- Maintain good arm mechanics
- Do not sink into the hips at the take-off and landing phases
- Land on the balls of the feet
- Do not fall back on the heels

Sets and reps
2 sets of 8 reps with 1 min recovery between each set.

Variations/progressions
- Single jumps over the hurdle and back
- Single jump over the hurdle with 180-degree twist (NB: practise twisting to both sides)
- Lateral single jumps – use both sides to jump off
- Ball can be thrown to the player to catch on landing
- Wicketkeeper should perform these drills with pads, helmet and gloves on

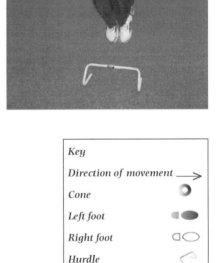

Key	
Direction of movement	⟶
Cone	◓
Left foot	◖●
Right foot	◗○
Hurdle	⌒

Figure 2.8(a) Two-footed single jump

Figure 2.8(b) Two-footed single jump with 180° twist

Figure 2.8(c) Two-footed lateral single jump

RUNNING FORM –
MULTIPLE HOPS AND JUMPS

Aim

To develop maximum control while taking off and landing. To develop controlled directional power.

Area/equipment

Indoor or outdoor area. Place 6–8 hurdles of either 7 or 12 inches in height at 2-foot intervals in a straight line.

Description

Players jump forwards over each hurdle in quick succession until all hurdles have been cleared, then walk back to the start and repeat the drill.

Key teaching points

- Use quick, rhythmic arm mechanics
- Do not sink into the hips at the take-off and landing phases
- Land and take off from the balls of the feet
- Stand tall and look straight ahead
- Maintain control
- Gradually build up the speed

Sets and reps

2 sets of 6 reps with 1 minute recovery between each set.

Variations/progressions

- Lateral jumps (see Fig 2.9(a))
- Jumps with 180-degree twist (see Fig. 2.9(b))
- Hop over the hurdles, balance, and then repeat (see Fig. 2.9(c))
- Use light handweights – for the last rep of each of these sets, perform the drill without the weights as a contrast
- Two forward jumps and one back
- Perform drills with a ball in the hand

Key	
Direction of movement	$\longrightarrow$
Cone	
Left foot	
Right foot	
Hurdle	

MULTIPLE HOPS AND JUMPS cont.

Figure 2.9(a) Lateral jumps

Figure 2.9(b) Jumps with 180° twist

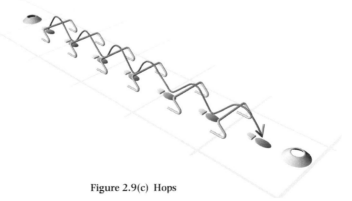

Figure 2.9(c) Hops

DRILL

RUNNING FORM –
STRIDE FREQUENCY AND LENGTH

Aim

To practise the transfer from the acceleration phase to the increase in stride frequency and length required when running. To develop an efficient leg cycle, rhythm, power, foot placement, deceleration, control and balance. To practise throwing and catching while under pressure.

Area/equipment

Indoor or outdoor area 40–60 yards long. Place 12 coloured stride frequency canes, marker dots or sticks at 2-, 3-, 4-, 5- and 6-foot intervals flat on the ground in a straight line (see Fig. 2.10). Sets of stumps should be placed 2 feet in front of the first cane and 2 feet after the last cane.

Description

Player 1 starts from behind the set of stumps at one end of the course. He/she will step round the stump and begin to accelerate down the stride frequency canes. The canes are laid out so that the initial stages for the run develop acceleration, therefore they are closer together; in the middle the canes are further apart, to develop stride length. The final few canes are closer together again to develop deceleration. Player 1, on reaching the end of the canes, will now decelerate. As he/she is about to reach the set of stumps at that end, Player 2, who is standing behind the stumps, throws the ball out at an angle along the ground. Player 1 now reaccelerates to field the ball and return it to Player 2 who has now moved to stand behind the stumps at that end.

Key teaching points

- Do not overstride
- Work off the balls of the feet
- Try to develop and maintain a rhythm
- Keep eyes and head up as if looking over a fence
- Maintain correct movement mechanics
- Maintain an upright posture
- Stay focused
- Alter distances between the canes for different ages and heights

Sets and reps

1 set of 4 reps.

Variations/progressions

- Bowlers to work through the grid with a ball in the hand
- The drill can be continuous by starting from both ends

Key	
Cone	
Stick	

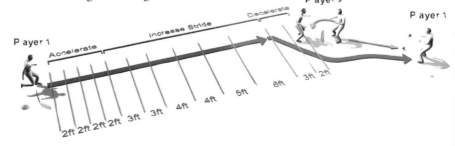

Figure 2.10 Stride frequency and length stick grid

DRILL
RUNNING FORM –
STRIDE FREQUENCY AND LENGTH (ADVANCED)

Aim
To practise the transfer from the acceleration phase to the increase in stride frequency and length required when running. To develop an efficient leg cycle, rhythm, power, foot placement, deceleration, control and balance. To practise throwing and catching while under pressure in a more complex and advanced situation.

Area/equipment
Indoor or outdoor area 40–60 yards long. Place 2 lines of 12 coloured stride frequency canes, marker dots or sticks at 2-, 3-, 4-, 5- and 6-foot intervals flat on the ground in a straight line, 10 yards apart (see Fig. 2.11). A set of stumps should be placed in the middle between the 2 lines of stride frequency canes. Marker dots should be placed at the beginning of each line of canes.

Description
Two players (1 and 2) simultaneously commence their run down the stride frequency canes. As they near the end, the coach, standing 15–20 yards away between the lines of canes, throws the ball along the ground at an angle away from Player 1. Player 1 now runs to field the ball, while Player 2 turns and accelerates to the stumps situated between the sets of canes. Player 1, on fielding the ball, throws the ball over the stumps to Player 2 who touches the stumps then returns the ball to the coach. The drill is then repeated on the other side.

Key teaching points
- Do not overstride
- Work off the balls of the feet
- Try to develop and maintain a rhythm
- Keep the eyes and head up as if looking over a fence
- Maintain correct movement mechanics
- Maintain an upright posture
- Stay focused
- Alter distances between strides for different ages and heights

Sets and reps
1 set of 4 reps.

Variations/progressions
- Bowlers to work through the grid with ball a in their hand
- The drill can be continuous by starting from both ends

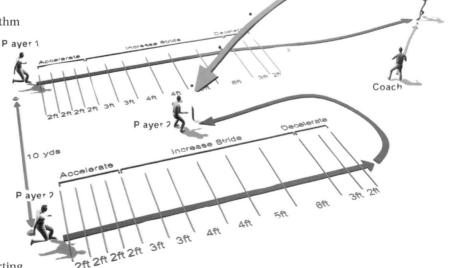

Figure 2.11 Stride frequency and length stick grid (advanced drill)

RUNNING FORM –
DRILL FIELDING WITH A BALL

Aim
To maintain good movement mechanics, balance and co-ordination when faced with cricket-specific movements and techniques and also to improve decision-making ability.

Area/equipment
Indoor or outdoor area. Place 8 hurdles in a straight line at 2-foot intervals. Place a marker at the start of one end and a set of stumps at the other end approximately 2 yards away from the last hurdle. Cricket balls.

Description
The coach stands just behind the stumps. Players perform a mechanics drill through the hurdles and, on clearing the final hurdle, accelerate onto the ball that has been rolled out at an angle away from the stumps by the coach. The player fields the ball and throws it back to the coach. (See Fig. 2.12)

Key teaching points
- Maintain correct movement mechanics
- Stay focused by looking ahead
- Fire the arms explosively when accelerating to the cricket ball

Sets and reps
3 sets of 6 reps. NB: the sets should be made up of various mechanics drills.

Variations/progressions
- On clearing the final hurdle, the ball is thrown at various heights into the air for the player to run, catch and throw back to the coach
- The player performs lateral mechanics drills with their back to the coach. The coach also works laterally approximately 2 yards away from the player. The coach throws the ball at various angles away from the player, so the player must turn and accelerate to field the ball

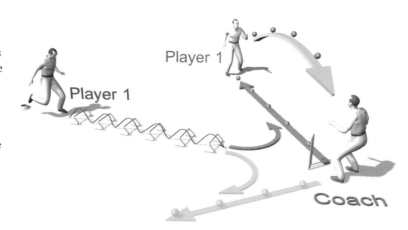

Figure 2.12 Fielding with a ball

DRILL   *RUNNING FORM – FIELDING DRILL*

Aim
To develop and maintain a high level of running performance while under pressure in the field.

Area/equipment
Large outdoor or indoor area of 40–60 yards. Place 16 hurdles in a line, the first 8 hurdles 2 feet apart, then a 5-yard gap, then the next line of 8 hurdles continues at 2 feet apart. Marker A is placed at the start 1 yard away from the first hurdle and marker B is placed between hurdles 8 and 9. A set of stumps is placed 2 yards away from the final hurdle. Cricket balls.

Description
From marker A Player 1 with a ball in his hand performs a drill down the first set of hurdles. Player 2 waits at marker B for Player 1 to reach the centre gap. As Player 1 clears the final hurdle, Player 2 throws the ball out at an angle to the left or right of the centre gap, then immediately turns and commences a drill down the second set of hurdles towards the stumps. On clearing the final hurdle, Player 2 accelerates behind the stump; Player 1, who has accelerated off to field the ball, now throws it back to Player 2 who removes the bails.

Key teaching points
- Maintain correct arm mechanics
- Work off the balls of the feet
- Try to develop and maintain a rhythm
- Keep the eyes and head up and look ahead
- Maintain an upright posture
- Keep the hips square

Sets and reps
4 sets of 4 reps.

Variations/progressions
- Perform the drills laterally
- Player 2 to throw 2 cricket balls for Player 1 to retrieve

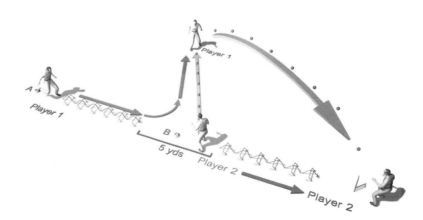

Figure 2.13 Fielding drill

DRILL RUNNING FORM – HURDLE MIRROR DRILLS

Aim
To improve the performance of drills under pressure. To improve random agility, balance and co-ordination.

Area/equipment
Indoor or outdoor area. Mark out a grid with 2 lines of 8 hurdles, with 2 feet between each hurdle and 2 yards between each line of hurdles.

Description
Players face each other while performing drills up and down the lines of hurdles. One player initiates the movements while the partner attempts to mirror those movements. Players can perform both lateral and linear mirror drills. (See Fig. 2.14(a).)

Key teaching points
- Stay focused on your partner
- The player mirroring should try to anticipate the lead player's movements
- Maintain correct arm mechanics

Sets and reps
Each player performs 3 sets of 30-second work periods, with a 30-second recovery between each work period.

Variations/progressions
- First-to-the-ball drill – as above, except a cricket ball is placed between the 2 lines of hurdles. The proactive partner commences the drill as normal then accelerates to the ball, fields it and sprints past the end cones. The reactive player attempts to beat the proactive player to the ball (see Fig. 2.14(b))
- Lateral drills performed as above – players work in pairs with only 2 hurdles per player. This is effective for improving the short, lateral steps used in fielding (see Fig. 2.14(c))

Figure 2.14(a) Hurdle mirror drills

HURDLE MIRROR DRILLS cont.

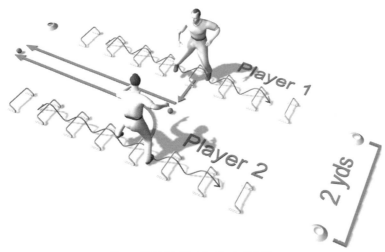

Figure 2.14(b) First-to-the-ball drill

Figure 2.14(c) Lateral drills

DRILL   RUNNING FORM – CURVED ANGLE RUN

Aim

To develop controlled, explosive fast feet while running on a curved angle, particularly around the boundary.

Area/equipment

Indoor or outdoor area. Place 10 hurdles in a curved formation, 2 feet apart. Place a marker at each end, approximately 2 yards from the first and last hurdles respectively.

Description

Players perform running drill as already described (the Dead-leg run, Lateral stepping or Leading leg run) with the same leg leading over each hurdle.

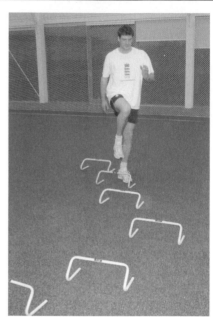

Key teaching points

- Work both the left and right sides
- The knee-lifts should be no more than 45 degrees
- Use short, sharp steps
- Maintain powerful arm mechanics
- Maintain an upright posture
- Look ahead at all times

Sets and reps

Each player performs 1 set of 6 reps with a 30-second recovery between each rep.

Variations/progressions

- Introduce the cricket ball
- Introduce tighter curves
- Perform immediately after straight-run hurdle work

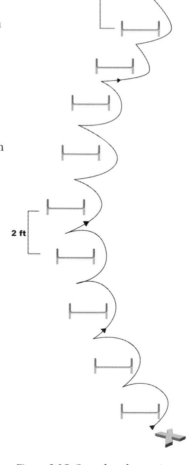

Key

Direction of run	→
Cone	O
Hurdle	⊓
Player	✕

Figure 2.15 Curved angle running

DRILL RUNNING FORM – COMPLEX MECHANICS

Aim

To prevent players resorting to bad habits, particularly when under pressure. To challenge players, when placed in game-like pressure situations, to maintain good running form even in the most difficult and demanding of situations.

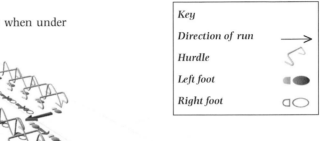

Key	
Direction of run	→
Hurdle	
Left foot	
Right foot	

Area/equipment

Indoor or outdoor area. Place 4 hurdles in a straight line with 2 feet between each hurdle. The next 4 hurdles are set slightly to one side and the final 4 hurdles are placed back in line with the original 4.

Description

Players perform a dead-leg run over the hurdles with the dead leg changing over the 4 centre hurdles, and return to the start by performing the drill over the hurdles in the opposite direction. See Figure 2.16(a).

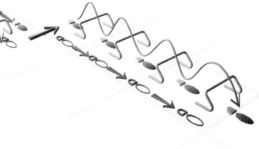

Key teaching points

- Maintain correct arm mechanics
- Work off the balls of the feet
- Try to develop and maintain a rhythm
- Keep eyes and head up and look ahead
- Maintain an upright posture
- Keep the hips square

Figure 2.16(a) Complex mechanics drills

Sets and reps

4 sets of 4 reps.

Variations/progressions

- Perform the drill laterally moving both forwards and backwards to cross the centre 4 hurdles (see Fig. 2.16(b))
- Place the hurdles in a cross formation and perform drills up to the centre and sideways, left or right, up or across
- Introduce players from other sides/groups
- Once the drill is mastered, players should work with a ball in their hand

Figure 2.16(b) Complex lateral mechanics drills

ENDURANCE TRAINING –
INTERVAL RUNNING FOR BATSMEN

Area/equipment
- Indoor or outdoor area, 22-yard grid, 11-yard half-way markers.
- Marker dots

Description
This SAQ cricket-specific batsman run is interval running based on a six-ball over and recovery between overs. The intervals are dictated by the coach who nominates the type of bowler for each over, i.e. for the slow bowler, the interval between balls is shorter (30-seconds). For the medium-pace bowler, who takes a medium run-up, the recovery of 40 seconds between balls is slightly longer, and for the fast bowler, whose long run-up dictates that the intervals between each ball is much longer than for the slow bowler, the recovery interval is 50 seconds. The interval between balls can be changed by the coach according to the intensity and time of season in training. Mark out a 22-yard grid representing the length of the wicket. Place a marker down the centre to represent the half-way mark of 11 yards. Overs are compromised of 6 balls, also no balls and overthrows can be added to additional runs. Although it is called a cricket-specific *batsman* run it is excellent for all cricketers.

This is the key:
- No runs – the player jogs to the centre and walks back to the start. This represents backing up the batsman.
- One run (22 yards)
- Two runs (44 yards)
- Three runs (66 yards)
- Four runs (88 yards)

If the coach calls 'overthrow' while the batsman is running, an additional 22 yards is to be run, i.e. the coach calls '3 runs', then on the final run he calls 'overthrow', whereupon the batsman will run the additional run. Therefore, 88 yards will have been completed. When a no ball is called by the coach, then an extra ball is added to the over. Runs can be taken on a no ball. Recovery between overs can be varied between 1 and 2 minutes depending on the time of season.

The run starts by the coach indicating the type of bowler, e.g. 'slow'; he then informs the player that the bowler is about to run up and then he calls the number of runs that the batsman has scored. If the batsman scores 1, the player runs 22 yards to the other side, then has a recovery of 30 seconds. The coach now may call 'no runs'; the batsman will jog to the centre mark and then walk back. On the third ball, the coach may call '3 runs', which will indicate that the batsman will run 3 × 22 yards and so on. The number of overs to be bowled can be varied depending on the time of season and the level of intensity required. Also, intensity can be changed by varying the combination of bowler at each end, i.e. slow, medium, fast and so on.

Sets and reps
The following are programmes that can be used:

PROGRAMME 1   8 OVERS PRE–SEASON TRAINING (EARLY)

Over 1, fast bowler (50-second recovery between each ball)
1 run
2 runs
1 run
2 runs
1 run
1 run   2-minute recovery   8 × 22   176 yards total

Over 2, fast bowler
2 runs
1 run
3 runs
1 run
2 runs
3 runs   2-minute recovery   12 × 22   264 yards total

Over 3, fast bowler
1 run
1 run
4 runs
2 runs
2 runs
1 run   2-minute recovery   11 × 22   242 yards total

Over 4, slow bowler (30-second recovery between each ball)
2 runs
2 runs
1 run
3 runs
3 runs
3 runs   2-minute recovery   14 × 22   308 yards total

Over 5, medium-pace bowler (40-second recovery between each ball)
1 run
1 run
2 runs
3 runs
2 runs
1 run, no ball
1 run, extra ball   2-minute recovery   11 × 22   242 yards total

PROGRAMME 2 • 10 OVERS cont.

Over 6, slow bowler

1 run
4 runs
2 runs
3 runs
2 runs
5 runs   2-minute recovery   17 × 22   374 yards total

Over 7, medium-pace bowler

1 run
2 runs
1 run
1 run
3 runs
1 run   2-minute recovery   9 × 22   198 yards total

Over 8, slow bowler

3 runs
2 runs
1 run
1 run
4 runs
2 runs   2-minute recovery   13 × 22   286 yards total

Over 9, slow bowler

1 run
1 run
5 runs, 2 overthrows
2 runs
1 run
2 runs   2-minute recovery   14 × 22   308 yards total

Over 10, slow bowler

2 runs
5 runs
2 runs
4 runs
3 runs
4 runs   2-minute recovery   20 × 22   440 yards total

TOTAL 2,860 yards.

3-minute recovery before next activity

PROGRAMME 3 • 12 OVERS

Over 1, fast bowler

1 run
1 run
4 runs
2 runs
2 runs
1 run   2-minute recovery   11 × 22   242 yards total

Over 2, fast bowler

1 run
1 run
2 runs
2 runs
1 run
No run   2-minute recovery   8 × 22   176 yards total

Over 3, fast bowler

No run
3 runs
2 runs
1 run
2 runs
2 runs, no ball
2 runs, extra ball   2-minute recovery   13 × 22   286 yards total

Over 4, medium-pace bowler

2 runs
2 runs
1 run
3 runs
3 runs
3 runs   2-minute recovery   14 × 22   308 yards total

Over 5, medium-pace bowler

1 run
1 run
2 runs
3 runs
2 runs
1 run, no ball
1 run, extra ball   2-minute recovery   11 × 22   242 yards total

PROGRAMME 3 • 12 OVERS cont.

Over 6, medium-pace bowler

1 run
2 runs
1 run
1 run
3 runs
1 run   2-minute recovery   9 × 22   198 yards total

Over 7, slow bowler

1 run
4 runs
2 runs
3 runs
2 runs
5 runs   2-minute recovery   17 × 22   374 yards total

Over 8, slow bowler

3 runs
2 runs
1 run
1 run
4 runs
2 runs   2-minute recovery   13 × 22   286 yards total

Over 9, medium-pace bowler

1 run
1 run
5 runs, 2 overthrows
2 runs
1 run
2 runs   2-minute recovery   14 × 22   308 yards total

Over 10, slow bowler

2 runs
5 runs
2 runs
4 runs
3 runs
4 runs   2-minute recovery   20 × 22   440 yards total

PROGRAMME 3 • 12 OVERS cont.

Over 11, fast bowler

1 run, no ball
No run
2 runs
3 runs
1 run
No run, no ball
3 runs, extra ball
3 runs, extra ball   2-minute recovery   15 × 22   330 yards total

Over 12, slow bowler

2 runs
3 runs
No run
3 runs, 1 overthrow
1 run
2 runs   2-minute recovery   13 × 22   286 yards total

TOTAL 3,476 yards

3-minute recovery before next activity

ENDURANCE TRAINING –
INTERVAL RUNNING FOR FIELDERS

This running session is excellent for developing endurance and maintaining a player's explosive speed and reactions. It is also movement-specific and challenging, thus keeping the players interested and motivated. Remember, this type of work is all about quality not quantity. Focus should be on intensity levels and recovery, not one-paced slogs.

Aim
To improve endurance

Area/equipment
Mark out an indoor or outdoor grid starting with centre markers 22 yards apart to represent the wicket, then place inner markers closely around the wicket and corresponding outer markers at alternating distances of 20 and 30 yards in the outfield. (See Fig. 2.17.)

Description
Two players who are the batsmen stand at each end of the wicket while other players are spread around the markers in the outfield. On the coach's call the batsmen will run 2 runs, which is 44 yards up and down the wicket working on a 1:3 recovery ratio. This means if the runs take 10 seconds the batsmen are allowed 30 seconds recovery before the next run. The batsmen will run up and back 44 yards 6 times – the equivalent of one 6-ball over – a total of 264 yards. At the same time the outfielders, on the same call of the coach, will accelerate from the outfield to the infield markers situated near the wicket. While the batsmen are recovering between runs, the fielders will have an active recovery walking in a clockwise direction quickly back to the next outfield marker. Fielders will run the equivalent of 150 yards plus 150 yards walk-back recovery. On the completion of a 6-ball over there is a 2-minute recovery for all players, the batsmen are swapped with 2 fielders and the drill recommences. The size of the squad will determine the number of markers set out in the outfield. If there is an odd number, more than 2 batsmen can be used in the centre runs.

Key teaching points
■ Maintain quality running form at all times

Sets and reps
A player will cover the following distances:

6 overs   264 yards as a batsman (1 over)
           750 yards as a fielder (5 overs)

Total distance covered is 1,014 yards high-intensity interval running, with 750 yards active recovery.

INTERVAL RUNNING FOR FIELDERS cont.

10 overs   264 yards as a batsman (1 over)
           1,350 yards as a fielder (9 overs)

Total distance covered is 1,614 yards high-intensity interval running,
1,350 yards active walk-back recovery.

Variations/progressions
■ Vary recovery times
■ Players to perform centre run more than once

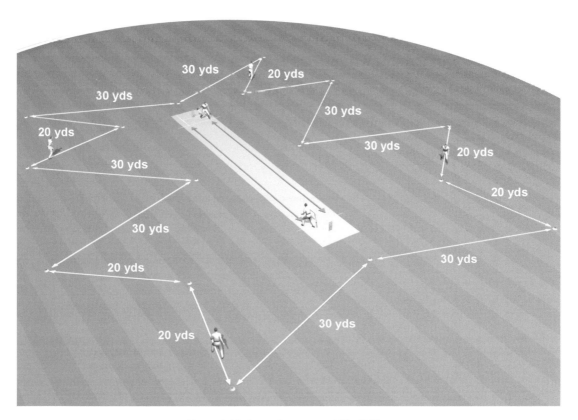

Figure 2.17 Interval running grid for fielders

INTERVAL RUNNING SESSIONS (A) cont.

SESSION 4

1 × 150 m	Work/rest ratio of 1:3
1 × 100 m	Work/rest ratio of 1:3
1 × 50 m	Work/rest ratio of 1:3
2 × 25 m	Work/rest ratio of 1:3
4 × 10 m	Work/rest ratio of 1:3
5 × 10 m	Work/rest ratio of 1:3

Players should complete session 4 five times with a full 3-minute recovery between each set.

SESSION 5

10 × 20 m	Work/rest ratio of 1:2
5 × 50 m	Work/rest ratio of 1:3
6 × 25 m	Work/rest ratio of 1:2
3 × 100 m	Work/rest ratio of 1:3
4 × 75 m	Work/rest ratio of 1:3
10 × 15 m	Work/rest ratio of 1:1.5

SESSION 6

5 × 10 m	Work/rest ratio of 1:1.5
10 × 15 m	Work/rest ratio of 1:1.5
5 × 100 m	Work/rest ratio of 1:2.5
3 × 150 m	Work/rest ratio of 1:3
5 × 15 m	Work/rest ratio of 1:2
3 × 20 m	Work/rest ratio of 1:2

SESSION 7

5 × 80 m	Work/rest ratio of 1:2.5
5 × 25 m	Work/rest ratio of 1:2
5 × 50 m	Work/rest ratio of 1:2
5 × 60 m	Work/rest ratio of 1:3
5 × 30 m	Work/rest ratio of 1:2

Variations/progressions

■ Different starting positions
■ Markers to be set out at different angles

ENDURANCE TRAINING –

DRILL INTERVAL RUNNING SESSIONS (B)

Aim
To develop a player's ability to recover and repeat short explosive bouts of activities.

Area/equipment
Indoor or outdoor area, markers placed as described in the sets and reps.

Description
Players to run at a high intensity as described in the sets and reps.

Sets and reps
SESSION 1

5 × 80 m	Work/rest ratio of 1:2 (based on time)
5 × 25 m	Work/rest ratio of 1:2
5 × 50 m	Work/rest ratio of 1:2
5 × 60 m	Work/rest ratio of 1:2
5 × 30 m	Work/rest ratio of 1:2

SESSION 2

6 × 40 m	Work/rest ratio of 1:2
6 × 50 m	Work/rest ratio of 1:2
6 × 30 m	Work/rest ratio of 1:2
6 × 20 m	Work/rest ratio of 1:2
20 × 5 m	Immediate turn around and repeat

SESSION 3

5 × 50 m	Work/rest ratio of 1:2
5 × 80 m	Forwards for 40 m, backwards for 10 m and then forwards for 30 m. Work/rest ratio of 1:2.5, work/rest ratio of 1:2
5 × 40 m	Work/rest ratio of 1:2
5 × 80 m	Forwards for 40 m, backwards for 10 m and then forwards for 30 m. Work/rest ratio of 1:2.5, work/rest ratio of 1:2
5 × 50 m	Work/rest ratio of 1:2

SESSION 4

6 × 40 m	Forwards for 20 m, turn and run for 10 m, turn again and run for 10 m to finish
8 × 20 m	To be completed from different start positions
6 × 40 m	As above set 1
8 × 20 m	As above set 2
6 × 30 m	Forwards for 10 m, backwards for 10 m and then forwards for 10 m to finish

INTERVAL RUNNING SESSIONS (B) cont.

All of session 4 to be completed on a work/rest ratio of 1:2. Sets 2 and 4 in session 4 are to be completed from different start positions, which you should select from the options below. Be sure to vary them within the set and from session to session.

Variations/progressions

- Forward split stance – be sure to alternate the leading leg
- Forward parallel stance – again be sure to alternate the foot that makes the first step
- Sideways stance – turn and go, bearing the above point in mind
- Backwards stance – turn and go, working on turning on both shoulders

Within each session take a full 3-minute recovery between each set.

CHAPTER 3 INNERVATION

FAST FEET, AGILITY, CO-ORDINATION, BALANCE AND CONTROL FOR CRICKET

Innervation is the transition stage from warm-up and mechanics to periods of high-intensity work that activate the neural pathways. Using Fast Foot Ladders, dance-like patterns such as twists, jumps and turns are all introduced, increasing the rate of firing in the neuro-muscular system.

Once the basic footwork patterns have been mastered, more advanced, cricket-specific footwork drills that require speed, co-ordination and agility can be introduced. The key here is to speed up the movement techniques without compromising the quality of players' movement mechanics. The innervation drills in this chapter progress from simple footwork patterns to complex cricket-specific drills that include fielding, batting and bowling.

DRILL FAST FOOT LADDER – SINGLE RUN

Aim
To develop linear fast feet with control, precision and power.

Area/equipment
Indoor or outdoor area. Use a Fast Foot Ladder – ensure that this is the correct ladder for the type of surface being used.

Description
Players cover the length of the ladder by placing a foot in each ladder space (see Fig. 3.1(a)). Return to the start by jogging back beside the ladder.

Key teaching points
- Maintain correct running form and mechanics
- Start slowly and gradually increase the speed
- Maintain an upright posture
- Stress that quality not quantity is important

Sets and reps
3 sets of 4 reps with 1-minute recovery between each set.

Variations/progressions
- Single lateral step – as above but performed laterally (see Fig. 3.1(b))
- In-and-out – moving sideways along the ladder stepping into and out of each ladder space, i.e. both feet in then both feet out (see Fig. 3.1(c))
- 'Icky Shuffle' – sidestepping movement into and out of each ladder space while moving forwards (see Fig. 3.1(d))
- Double run – perform as single run above but with both feet in each ladder space (see Fig. 3.1(e))
- Hopscotch (see Fig. 3.1(f))
- Single-space jumps – two-footed jumps into and out of each ladder space (see Fig. 3.1(g))
- Two forwards and one back (see Fig. 3.1(h))
- 'Spotty dogs' (see Fig. 3.1(i))
- 'Twist again' (see Fig. 3.1(j))
- Hops in-and-out (see Fig. 3.1(k))
- Carioca (see Fig. 3.1(l))

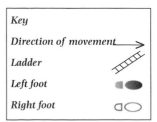

Key

Direction of movement

Ladder

Left foot

Right foot

FAST FOOT LADDER cont.

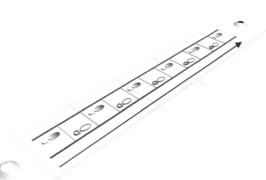

Figure 3.1(a) Single runs

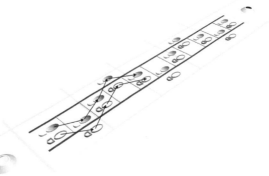

Figure 3.1(d) 'Icky shuffle'

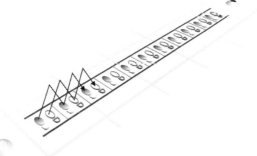

Figure 3.1(b) Single lateral step

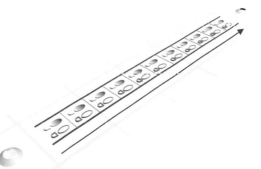

Figure 3.1(e) Double run

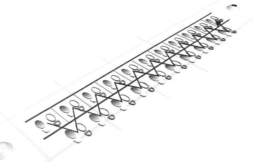

Figure 3.1(c) In-and-out

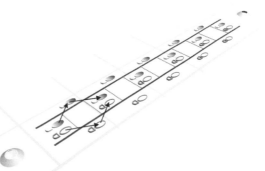

Figure 3.1(f) Hopscotch

FAST FOOT LADDER cont.

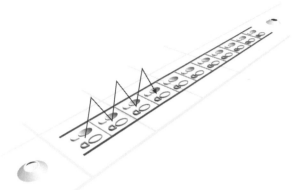

Figure 3.1(g) Single-space jumps

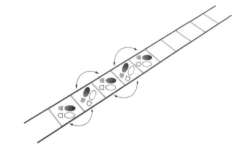

Figure 3.1(j) 'Twist again'

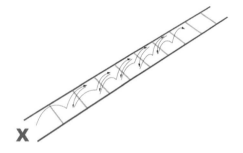

X

Figure 3.1(h) Two forwards and one back

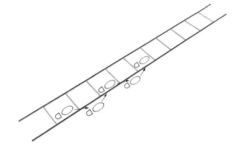

Figure 3.1(k) Hops in-and-out

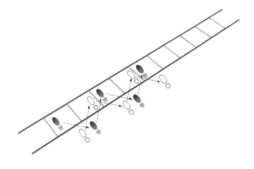

Figure 3.1(i) 'Spotty dogs'

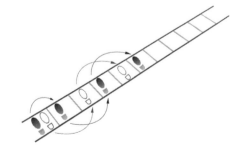

Figure 3.1(l) Carioca

DRILL   *FAST FOOT LADDER – T FORMATION*

Aim
To develop speed of acceleration when chasing a ball or setting off for a run. To develop the transfer from linear running to lateral running needed when turning and receiving a ball.

Area/equipment
Indoor or outdoor area. Place 2 ladders in a T formation, with 1 marker at the start and a set of stumps 1 yard away from each end of the head of the T. (See Fig. 3.2.)

Description
Player 1 accelerates down the ladder using single steps. On reaching the ladder crossing the end, Player 1 moves laterally either left or right using short lateral steps. On coming out of the ladder, Player 1 then turns and steps behind the stumps. Player 2 (the next player) throws the ball to Player 1 who simulates knocking the bails off. The drill is then repeated for the next player.

Key teaching points
- Maintain correct running form and mechanics
- Use a strong arm drive when transferring from linear to lateral steps
- Take short steps when turning; do not cross the feet
- Correct throwing and catching techniques to be used at all times

Sets and reps
3 sets of 4 reps with 1-minute recovery between each set (2 reps moving to the left and 2 to the right per set).

Variations/progressions
- Start with a lateral run and, upon reaching the end ladder, accelerate in a straight line forwards down the ladder, then change angle to get behind the stumps
- Mix and match previous Fast Foot Ladder drills described earlier

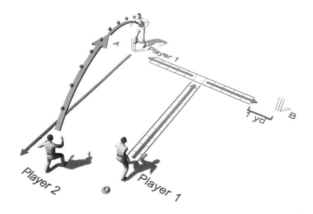

Figure 3.2 T formation throw and catch

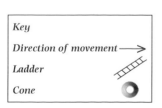

Key

Direction of movement ⟶

Ladder

Cone

DRILL FAST FOOT LADDER – CROSSOVER

Aim
To develop speed, agility and change of direction in a more pressured and crowded area. To improve reaction time, peripheral vision, timing and concentration.

Area/equipment
Large indoor or outdoor area. Place four ladders in a cross formation leaving a clear centre square of about 3 square yards. Place a marker 1 yard from the start of each ladder.

Description
Split the group into four equal teams and locate them at the start of each ladder. Players accelerate simultaneously down the ladder performing a single-step drill; on reaching the end of the ladder they accelerate across the centre square and join the end of the queue. They do not travel down this ladder. (See Fig. 3.3(a).)

Key teaching points
- Maintain correct running form and mechanics
- Keep the head and eyes up and be aware of other players, particularly around the centre area

Sets and reps
3 sets of 6 reps with 1-minute recovery between each set.

Variations/progressions
- At the end of the first ladder, sidestep to the right or left and join the appropriate adjacent ladder (see Fig. 3.3(b))
- Vary the Fast Foot Ladder drills performed down the first ladder
- Include a 360-degree turn in the centre square; this is effective for developing body and positional awareness

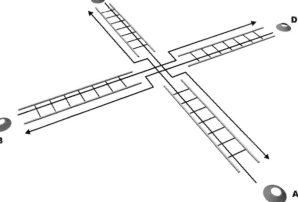

Figure 3.3(a) Crossover drill

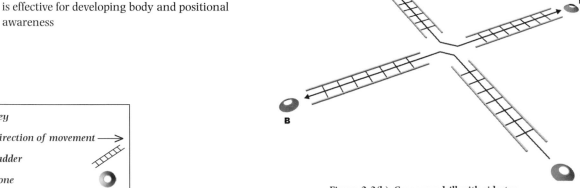

Figure 3.3(b) Crossover drill with sidestep

Key

Direction of movement ⟶

Ladder

Cone

DRILL   *FAST FOOT LADDER – MIRROR STEPS*

Aim
To develop explosive footwork patterns, reaction and response to complex movement situations, such as deflected cricket balls.

Area/equipment
Indoor or outdoor area. Use one 15-foot section of ladder.

Description
Player 1 and Player 2 stand opposite each other on either side of the ladder. Starting in the middle, Player 1 moves laterally and randomly steps in and out of the ladder. Player 2 responds by mirroring as quickly and as accurately as possible the movements of Player 1. (See Fig. 3.4.)

Key teaching points
- Maintain correct lateral running form and mechanics
- Use short, sharp, explosive steps
- Work off the balls of the feet
- Use a strong arm drive
- Always keep the hips square

Sets and reps
3 sets of 2 reps with a 15-second rest between reps and a 2-minute recovery between each set. NB: In each set each player should take the lead for 45 seconds.

Variations/progressions
Ball to be passed between players at regular frequencies to stimulate reactions.

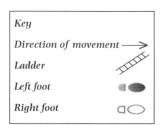

Key

Direction of movement ⟶

Ladder

Left foot

Right foot

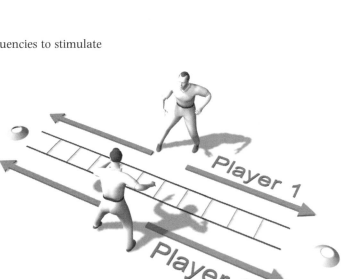

Figure 3.4 Fast feet mirror drill

DRILL

FAST FOOT LADDER –
WITH A CATCH AND THROW

Aim
To develop fast feet, balance, co-ordination, speed and agility while catching and throwing the cricket ball.

Area/equipment
Large indoor or outdoor area. Place a Fast Foot Ladder with markers about 1 yard away from each end.

Description
While Player 1 performs fast foot drills down the ladder either laterally or linearly, Player 2, standing 2 yards away from the ladder in a central position, throws the ball at different heights and angles, requiring that Player 1 catch and return the ball while in different positions and under different pressures. See Fig. 3.5.

Key teaching points
- Concentrate on good footwork patterns
- Ensure that correct technical skills are used when throwing and catching the cricket ball
- Ensure that the player performing the drill reverts to correct running form and mechanics after returning the ball

Sets and reps
3 sets of 6 reps with 1-minute recovery between each set.

Variations/progressions
Vary Fast Foot Ladder drills.

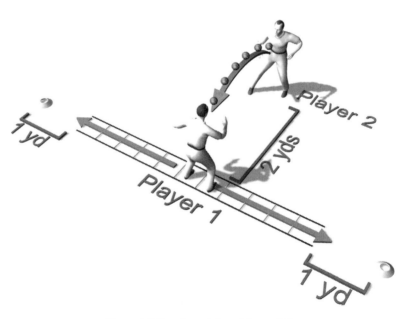

Figure 3.5 Fast feet catch and throw drill

DRILL	*FAST FOOT LADDER –* *WITH FIELDING AND THROWING*

Aim

To develop fast feet, balance, co-ordination and agility while fielding a ball in the outfield.

Area/equipment

Large indoor or outdoor area. Ladders, stumps and cricket ball. Place three sets of ladder sections next to each other, 2 yards apart at one end. The central ladder (Ladder A) will be straight and the ladders each side (B and C) will be angled away so that they are both 4 yards away at the other end from the centre Ladder A. Place a set of stumps 10 yards on from the end of Ladder A.

Description

Player 1 starts on ladder A, Players 2 and 3 start on B and C. On the coach's call all 3 players commence fast foot drills down the ladder. As they get near to the end, the coach, who is situated beyond the stumps, will roll a ball out to the left of ladder C. Player 1 accelerates from ladder A to cover the stumps, Player 2 accelerates from ladder B behind Player 1 to back up the throw and Player 3 accelerates out of ladder C, fields the ball and returns it to Player 1 over the stumps. See Fig. 3.6.

Key teaching points

- Maintain correct running form and mechanics
- Ensure that correct technical skills are used when players are throwing and catching the ball
- Players should communicate clearly, both visually and verbally

Sets and reps

3 sets of 6 reps with 1-minute recovery between each set, i.e. 3 reps as Player 1 and 3 reps as Player 2.

Variations/progressions

Vary the Fast Foot Ladder drills performed linearly and laterally by the players.

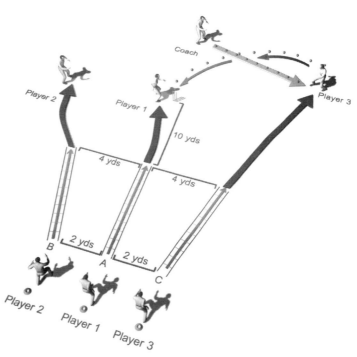

Figure 3.6 Fast feet fielding and throwing drill

DRILL
FAST FOOT LADDER –
LATERAL THROWING AND CATCHING

Aim
To develop fast foot combination work, balance, co-ordination, acceleration, timing, throwing and catching laterally under pressure.

Area/equipment
Large indoor or outdoor area. Place three sections of 15-foot ladder 5 yards apart and a stump 10 yards away at the end of each ladder as shown in Fig. 3.7.

Description
Player 1 accelerates down ladder A; Players 2 and 3 also accelerate down their corresponding ladders B and C. As Player 1 leaves ladder A, the coach (X) will throw a ball for the player to catch and then throw on to Player 2, who throws the ball to Player 3, who in turn catches and throws the ball to the second coach (Y). On completion of their throws the players accelerate to the end stumps A, B and C; coach Y now nominates out loud one of the players, and throws them the ball to catch and knock the stump. The players now jog back to the start, and the drill is repeated from the opposite side. See Fig. 3.7.

Key teaching points
- Maintain correct running form and mechanics
- Players should communicate
- Good timing of support runs is important
- Good throwing and catching techniques are to be used

Sets and reps
3 sets of 5 reps with a slow jog-back recovery between reps and a 2-minute recovery between each set.

Variations/progressions
- Vary the ladder drills
- Vary the type of throw
- Ball can be rolled so that it is fielded at ground level
- Vary the players' starting positions between the three ladders

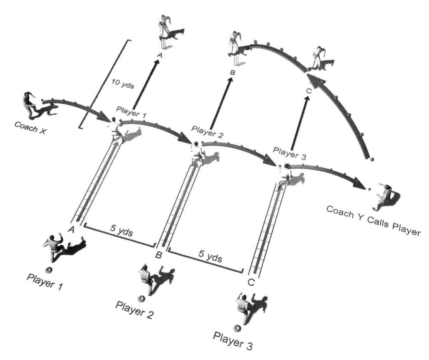

Figure 3.7 Fast feet lateral throwing and catching drill

DRILL   *FAST FOOT LADDER –*
FIELDING GIANT CROSSOVER

Aim
To develop fast feet, speed, agility, co-ordination, visual reaction and fielding skills, both with and without the ball.

Area/equipment
Large indoor or outdoor area. Place four ladders in a cross formation with 25 yards between them in the centre area. Use 2 or 4 cricket balls.

Description
Split the group into 4 equal teams and locate them at the start of each ladder A, B, C and D; two of the players have a cricket ball. Simultaneously, one player from each team accelerates down the ladder performing fast foot drills. The two players with the cricket balls pick them up, carry them across the centre then roll them to the oncoming players, who field the balls before rolling them to the next oncoming player. Having fielded the balls the players join the queue on the opposite side of the cross without travelling down the opposite ladder See Fig. 3.8.

Key teaching points
- This should be a continuous drill
- Maintain correct running form and mechanics
- Correct technical skills must be used when players are on the ball
- Players should use clear communication

Sets and reps
3 sets of 6 reps with 1-minute recovery between each set.

Variations/progressions
Instead of rolling the ball, introduce throw-and-catch.

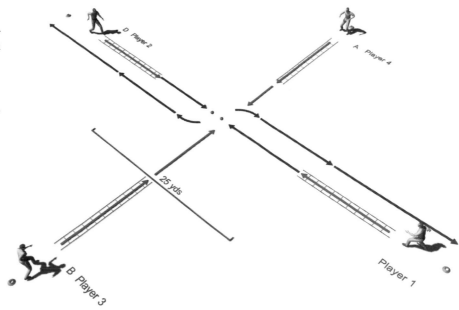

Figure 3.8 Fast feet giant crossover drill

DRILL
FAST FOOT LADDER –
FIELDING, BACK-UP AND THROW

Aim

To develop acceleration, balance and control while chasing a cricket ball in the deep outfield. To practise back-up running, throwing and catching.

Area/equipment

Large indoor or outdoor area, three ladders, two markers and cricket balls. Stagger two ladders A and B, 2 yards apart and one in front of the other. Lay a third ladder C, laterally, 5 yards in front of the starting ladder (see Fig. 3.9). Marker X is placed 20 yards away but directly in line with ladder A, and marker Y is placed 10 yards away laterally across from ladder C.

Description

Player 1 starts his/her run down ladder A and accelerates out of the ladder towards marker X. The coach, standing near marker X, rolls the ball towards it for Player 1 to field. Player 2 times his/her run to start after Player 1 has passed him/her on the inside and accelerates down ladder B to back-up Player 1. On reaching the ball, Player 1 flicks it up to Player 2, who catches the ball and throws it towards marker Y. Player 3, timing his/her run, accelerates down lateral ladder C and arrives at marker X in time to catch the ball, and then throws it back to the coach standing at marker X. See Fig. 3.9.

Key teaching points

- Maintain good arm mechanics
- Keep head and eyes up
- Use correct throwing and catching techniques

Sets and reps

3 sets of 6 reps with 1-minute recovery between each rep.

Variations/progressions

Vary ladder drills.

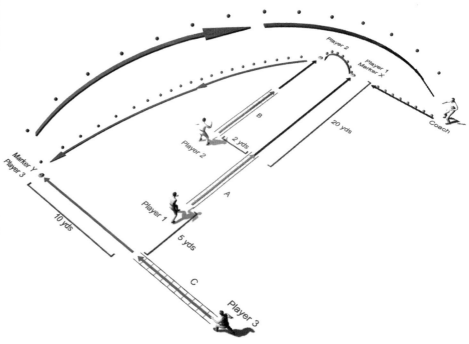

Figure 3.9 Fast feet fielding back-up and throw drill

CHAPTER 4 ACCUMULATION OF POTENTIAL

THE SAQ CRICKET CIRCUIT

This is the part of the continuum that brings together those areas of work already practised. Many of the mechanics and fast-foot drills are specific to developing a particular skill. In cricket the skills are rarely isolated but occur in quick succession or in combinations. An example of this is when a player runs at full speed after a ball hit towards the boundary, decelerates, scoops the ball up, changes direction and accelerates away while throwing the ball towards a wicket. Combinations of manoeuvres occur over different time-spans throughout a game of cricket.

Using ladders, hurdles, markers, poles and so on cricket-specific circuits can be used to develop programmed agility as well as to condition the player for this type of high intensity work.

This phase should not fatigue the players. Ensure a maximum recovery period between sets and reps.

DRILL — AGILITY RUNS – 4-CORNER BALL

Aim
To develop multi-directional explosive agility, turn mechanics and running mechanics both with and without the ball. Ideal for close fielders and for developing fast, controlled turns for batsmen.

Area/equipment
Indoor or outdoor area of about 10 square yards. Place 5 markers, one on each corner and one in the middle of the square, as shown in Fig. 4.1.

Description
Players start at the centre marker E, then accelerate out to and around marker A and back to marker E. Players then complete the drill by going out and around markers B, C and D (this is 1 repetition).

Key teaching points
■ Maintain correct running form and mechanics
■ Use strong arm mechanics both with and without the ball
■ Keep tight to the markers on the turns
■ Work off the balls of the feet

Sets and reps
3 sets of 2 reps with 1-minute recovery between reps and 2-minute recovery between sets.

Variations/progressions
■ Batsman runs up to the outer markers, turns sharply then sprints back to centre marker E
■ Place a ball on each outer marker A, B, C and D. Player sprints to the marker, scoops up the ball and returns it to marker E. This is continued for all four balls.

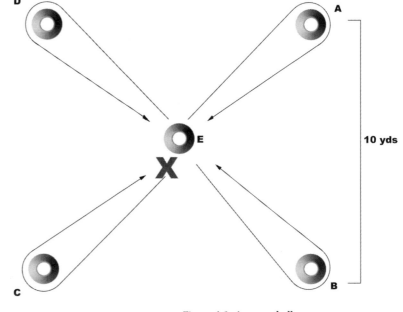

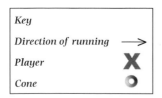

Key

Direction of running →

Player X

Cone ◯

Figure 4.1 4-corner ball

DRILL ZIGZAG RUNS

Aim
To develop fast, co-ordinated and controlled angled lateral runs.

Area/equipment
Indoor or outdoor area. Mark out a grid using 10–12 markers or poles in 2 lines of 5–6. Stagger them so that the line is a zigzag formation as shown in Fig. 4.2(a).

Description
Players run the zigzag formation, staying on the inside of the markers, and then walk back to the start before repeating the drill.

Key teaching points
- Maintain correct running form and mechanics
- Players must keep their hips facing the direction they are running
- Use short steps
- Do not skip
- Use good arm mechanics. NB: Arm mechanics are as vital in lateral movements as they are in linear movements; many players forget to use their arms when they are moving sideways

Sets and reps
3 sets of 6 reps with a walk-back recovery between each rep and a 1-minute recovery between each set.

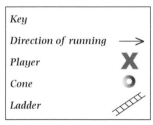

Variations/progressions
- Perform the drill backwards, performing the jockeying movement
- Players to go around each marker rather that staying on the inside of them
- Up-and-back – enter the grid sideways and move forwards to the first marker then backwards to the next, etc.
- Add a Fast Foot Ladder to the start and finish for acceleration and deceleration running (see Fig. 4.2(b))

Figure 4.2(a) Zigzag run

Figure 4.2(b) Ladder zigzag run

DRILL   *MOVEMENT CIRCUIT*

Aim
To develop running patterns likely to be encountered in a game of cricket.

Area/equipment
Markers, hurdles, Fast Foot Ladders and poles. These are all to be placed in a circuit within the area, as shown in Fig. 4.3(a).

Description
Players follow a direction that will take them through ladders, stepping and jumping over hurdles, sidestepping through markers, running backwards, jumping and turning. NB: one circuit should take the players 30–60 seconds to complete.

Key teaching point
Maintain correct running form/mechanics for all activities

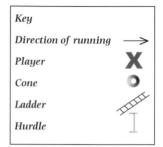

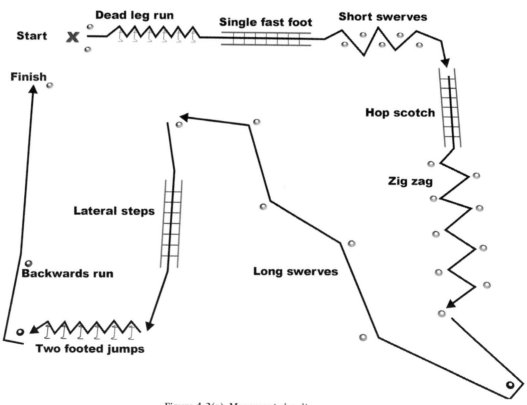

Figure 4.3(a) Movement circuit

MOVEMENT CIRCUIT cont.

Sets and reps

1 set of 6 reps with a varied recovery time between each rep depending on the stage in the season.

Variations/progressions

- Include throwing and catching, running with the bat and ball and curved boundary runs (see Fig. 4.3 (b))
- Vary the circuit and the drills on a regular basis, using imagination and cricket knowledge

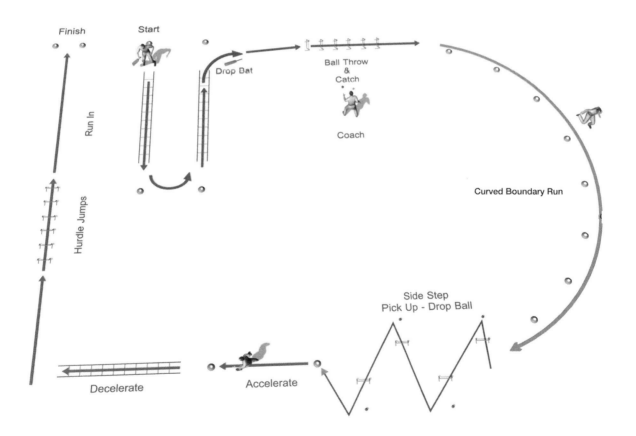

Figure 4.3(b) Movement circuit with curved boundary run

CRICKET-SPECIFIC
DRILL COMPETITIVE TEAM CIRCUIT

Aim
To develop cricket-specific movements and skills in a competitive and pressurised environment.

Area/equipment
Large indoor or outdoor area, ladder, hurdles, markers and cricket balls. Two identical circuits to be placed next to each other within the area.

Description
Players split into 2 teams, A and B. Players from each team start at the beginning of the circuit at the same time. They compete with each other as they perform the drills; on reaching the end the player picks up a ball placed at the final marker and throws it to his team member who is waiting at the start of the circuit; as soon as the ball is caught and returned the next team member commences the circuit. The ball is placed at the end marker ready for the next transfer. The drill continues until all team members have completed the circuit. The winning team is the one that finishes first. See Fig. 4.4.

Key teaching point
Maintain correct running form and mechanics for all activities. This is an excellent time for the coach to evaluate players' performance under pressure.

Sets and reps
2 sets of 3 reps with 1-minute recovery between sets.

Variation/progression
Vary drills within a circuit.

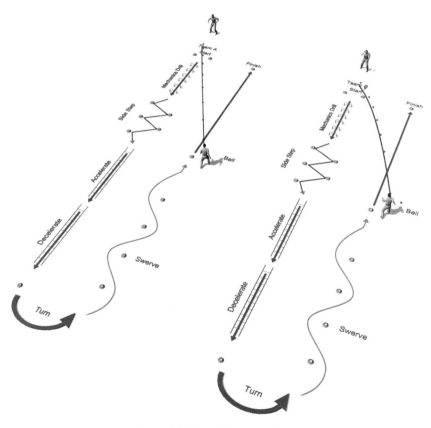

Figure 4.4 Competitive team circuit

CHAPTER 5 EXPLOSION

THREE-STEP MULTI-DIRECTIONAL ACCELERATION FOR CRICKET

The exercises outlined in the chapter have been designed to boost response times and develop multi-directional, explosive movements.

Programmable and random agility is trained using resisted and assisted high-quality plyometrics. Plyometrics exercises focus on the stretch-shortening cycle of the muscles involved, an action that is a central part of cricket performance. Plyometrics drills include drop-jumps, hops, skips and bounds. Plyometrics can be fun and challenging and adds variety to training sessions. However, there is potential for injury with these exercises so they must be performed using the correct technique and at the correct point in the training session.

Upper-body speed and power are also catered for with jelly-ball work-outs, which are effective for the type of strength required for throwing and batting. The power used for arm drive that improves running, speed and jumping height can be dramatically improved.

The crucial element in using explosive drills is the implementation of the 'contrast' phase. This simply means performing the drill without resistance for one or two reps immediately after performing it with resistance. These movements will naturally be more explosive and more easily remembered and reproduced over a period of time. The key is to ensure that quality not quantity is the priority. Efforts must be carefully monitored.

This is a time for high-intensity explosive action, not 'tongue-hanging out fatigue'!

DRILL SEATED FORWARD GET-UPS

Aim
To develop multi-directional explosive acceleration. To improve a player's ability to get up and accelerate all in one movement.

Area/equipment
Indoor or outdoor area of 20 square yards.

Description
Players sit on the floor, facing the direction they are going to run in, with legs straight out in front. On the signal from the coach, players get up as quickly as possible, accelerate for 10 yards and then slow down before jogging gently back to the start position.

Key teaching points
- Try to complete the drill in one smooth action
- Use correct running form and mechanics
- Do not stop between getting up and starting to run
- Get into an upright position and drive the arms as soon as possible
- Ensure the initial steps are short and powerful
- Do not overstride

Sets and reps
3 sets of 5 reps with a jog-back recovery between each rep and a 2-minute recovery between each set.

Variations/progressions
- Seated backward get-ups
- Seated sideways get-ups
- Lying get-ups from the front, back, left and right
- Kneeling get-ups
- Work in pairs and have get-up competitions chasing a ball
- Work in pairs with one player in front of the other and perform 'tag' get-ups

DRILL   LET-GOES

Aim
To develop multi-directional explosive acceleration.

Area/equipment
Indoor or outdoor area of 20 square yards; Viper Belt with hand leash.

Description
Player 1 wears the Viper Belt: he/she attempts to accelerate away in a straight line forwards while being resisted from behind by Player 2, who holds the hand leash to provide resistance. Player 2 maintains the resistance for a couple of seconds before releasing Player 1, who explodes away. (If a Viper Belt and hand leash are not available, Player 2 holds on to the shirt or top of Player 1.)

Key teaching points
- Player 1 should not lean or pull forward excessively
- Use short steps during the explosion and acceleration phases
- Use good arm drive
- Player 1 should adopt good running form and mechanics as soon as possible

Sets and reps
3 sets of 5 reps with a walk-back recovery between each rep and a 2-minute recovery between each set.

Variations/progressions
- Lateral let-goes
- Backward let-goes
- Let-goes with an acceleration onto a stationary ball
- Let-goes with an acceleration onto a moving ball

DRILL CHAIR GET-UPS

Aim
To develop explosive power for acceleration linearly and laterally.

Area/equipment
Indoor or outdoor area with plenty of room for deceleration – place a chair or stool and 5 markers as shown below in fig. 5.1.

Description
Players sit on a chair and, on the coach's signal, get up and move to the nominated marker as quickly as possible. On reaching the marker the player should decelerate and walk back to the start position.

Key teaching points
- Use an explosive arm drive when getting up
- Get into a correct running posture as quickly as possible
- Initial steps should be short and powerful
- Work off the balls of the feet

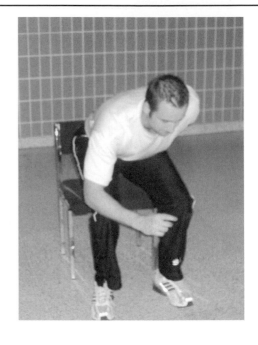

Sets and reps
3 sets of 10 reps with a walk-back recovery between each rep and a 2-minute recovery between each set.

Variations/progressions
Work in pairs: Player 1 to stand 1 or 2 yards away from the chair with two cricket balls and perform 'ball drops' by holding both arms out and dropping one of the balls for seated Player 2 to catch.

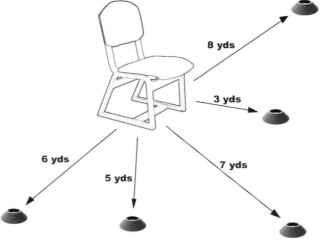

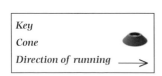

Key	
Cone	
Direction of running	→

Figure 5.1 Chair get-ups

8 yds

3 yds

6 yds

5 yds

7 yds

DRILL *FLEXI-CORD – BUGGY RUNS*

Aim
To develop multi-directional explosive acceleration.

Area/equipment
Indoor or outdoor area – ensure that there is plenty of room for safe deceleration. Viper Belt with a Flexi-cord attached at both ends by 2 anchor points. Place 3 markers in a line, 10 yards apart.

Description
Work in pairs: Player 1 wears the belt while Player 2 stands behind holding the Flexi-cord, with the hands looped in and over the cord (for safety purposes). Player 2 allows resistance to develop as Player 1 accelerates forward, then runs behind maintaining constant resistance over the first 10 yards. Both players need to decelerate over the second 10 yards. Player 1 removes the belt after the required number of reps and completes a solo contrast run. Repeat the drill but swap roles.

Key teaching points
- Player 1 must focus on correct running form and mechanics and explosive drive
- Player 2 works with Player 1, allowing the Flexi-cord to provide the resistance

Sets and reps
1 set of 6 reps plus 1 contrast run with a 30-second recovery between each rep and a 3-minute recovery before the next exercise.

Variations/progressions
- Lateral buggy run – Player 1 accelerates laterally for the first 2 yards before turning to cover the remaining distance linearly
- Player 2 to throw a ball over Player 1, who reacts and accelerates under resistance to field the ball

| DRILL | FLEXI-CORD – OUT AND BACK |

Aim
To develop short, explosive angled accelerated runs – ideal for close fielding development.

Area/equipment
Large indoor or outdoor area of 10 square yards would be ideal. Viper Belt with a Flexi-cord attached to 1 anchor point on the belt and a safety belt on the other end of the Flexi-cord. Five markers set up as in Fig. 5.2(a).

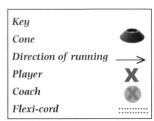

Key
Cone
Direction of running →
Player   X
Coach   ⊗
Flexi-cord   ::::::::::

Description
Work in pairs. Player 1 wears the Viper Belt, Player 2 stands directly behind Player 1 holding the Flexi-cord and wearing the safety belt. The Flexi-cord should be taut at this stage. Player 2 nominates a marker for Player 1, varying between the 3 markers for the required number of repetitions. Player 1 runs to the nominated marker, then returns to the start using short, sharp steps. Finish with a contrast run before swapping roles. See Fig. 5.2(b).

Key teaching points
- Focus on short, sharp explosive steps and a fast, powerful arm drive
- Maintain correct running form and mechanics
- Work off the balls of the feet
- Use short steps while returning to the start, and keep the weight forward

Start / Finish

3 yds

2 yds

2 yds

Figure 5.2(a) Flexi-cord out and back grid

Sets and reps
3 sets of 6 reps plus 1 contrast run per set, with a 3-minute recovery between each set. For advanced players, depending on the time of the season, increase to 10 reps.

Variations/progressions
- Perform the drill laterally
- Work backwards with short, sharp steps
- A third player or coach throws a ball for Player 1 to catch and return as they reach the designated marker (see Fig. 5.2(b))

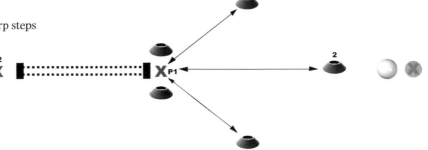

Figure 5.2(b) Flexi-cord out and back drill with ball

Aim

To develop explosive lateral fielding ability, particularly over the first few steps.

Area/equipment

Indoor or outdoor area. Viper Belt, Flexi-cords, cricket balls and 12 markers set up as shown in Fig. 5.3.

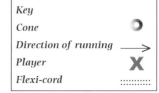

Description

Player 1, wearing the Viper Belt, runs a zigzag pattern between the markers. Player 2 works along the line between the 2 outside markers slightly behind Player 1 to ensure that the Flexi-cord does not get in the way of the arm mechanics. Work up and back along the line of zigzag markers. On completing the reps, Player 1 removes the belt and performs 1 contrast run.

Key teaching points

- Maintain correct running form and mechanics
- Use good technique for catching and throwing
- Use short steps when going backwards
- Keep the hips square
- Player 2 to move along with Player 1 concentrating on maintaining a constant distance, angle and resistance

Key	
Cone	◐
Direction of running	→
Player	**X**
Flexi-cord	··········

Sets and reps

3 sets of 8 reps plus 2 contrast runs and passes with a 3-minute recovery between each set.

Variations/progressions

- Introduce third player or coach who throws the ball to Player 1 during the drill
- Drill can be performed linearly
- By using a swivel belt or loosening the waist-size of the Viper Belt, batsmen can perform up-and-back runs with the bat

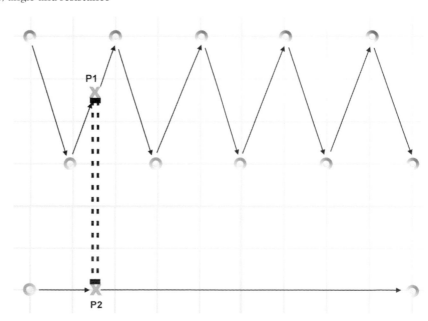

Figure 5.3 Flexi-cord lateral ball work

DRILL   *FLEXI-CORD – OVERSPEED*

Aim
To develop lightning-quick acceleration.

Area/equipment
Indoor or outdoor area. 4 markers and 1 Viper Belt with a Flexi-cord. Place the markers 3 yards apart in a T formation. (See Fig. 5.4.)

Description
Work in pairs. Player 1 wears the Viper Belt and faces Player 2, who holds the Flexi-cord and has the safety belt around their waist, i.e. the Flexi-cord will go from belly button to belly button. Player 1 stands at marker A, Player 2 stands at marker B and walks backwards away from Player 1, thereby increasing the cord's resistance. After stretching the cord for 4–5 yards, Player 1 accelerates towards Player 2 who then nominates marker C or D, requiring Player 1 to change direction explosively. Walk back to the start and repeat the drill.

Key teaching points
- Maintain correct running form and mechanics
- Control the running form and mechanics
- During the change of direction phase, shorten the steps and increase the rate of firing of the arms

Sets and reps
3 sets of 8 reps plus 1 contrast run with a 3-minute recovery between each set.

Variations/progressions
- Player 1 starts with a horizontal jump before accelerating away
- Introduce a ball, which is thrown for Player 1 to catch after the change of direction phase

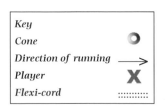

Key	
Cone	O
Direction of running	→
Player	X
Flexi-cord	··········

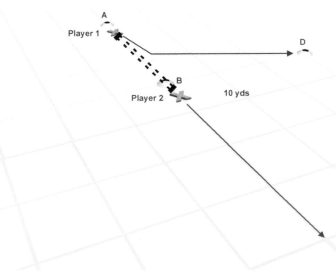

Figure 5.4 Flexi-cord overspeed

DRILL

SIDE-STEPPER –
RESISTED LATERAL RUNS

Aim
To develop explosive, controlled lateral patterns of running.

Area/equipment
Indoor or outdoor area. Side-Stepper. Place 10–12 markers in a zigzag pattern as shown in Fig. 5.5.

Description
The player wearing the Side-Stepper runs in a lateral zigzag between the markers down the length of the grid and, just, before a marker, extends the last step to increase the level of resistance. He/she then turns round and works back along the grid.

Key teaching points
- Maintain correct lateral running form and mechanics
- Do not sink into the hips when stepping off to change direction
- During the change of direction phase, increase arm speed to provide additional control

Sets and reps
3 sets of 6 reps plus 1 contrast run with a 3-minute recovery between each set.

Variations/progressions
- Perform the drill backwards
- Introduce a cricket ball on the change of direction phase
- Wicketkeeper to perform drills wearing pads, helmet and gloves

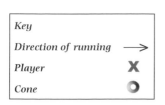

Key	
Direction of running	→
Player	**X**
Cone	**O**

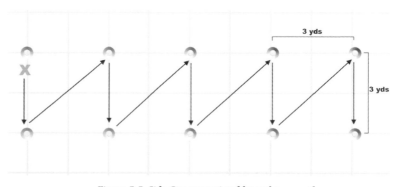

Figure 5.5 Side-Stepper resisted lateral runs grid

DRILL SIDE-STEPPER – JOCKEYING THROW AND CATCH

Aim
To develop the explosive lateral and angled movements used in fielding.

Area/equipment
Indoor or outdoor area. 6–8 markers. Side-Steppers. Mark out a channel about 22 yards long and 3 yards wide.

Description
Both players wear a Side-Stepper and face each other about 4 yards apart. Player 1 moves from right to left in a backwards pattern while Player 2 attempts to mirror the movements of Player 1. The ball is transferred between the players throughout the drill. On reaching the end of the grid the roles are reversed, with Player 1 moving forwards and Player 2 moving backwards.

Key teaching points
- Use quick, low steps, *not* high knees
- Do not skip or jump – one foot should be in contact with the floor at all times
- Try to keep the feet shoulder-width apart
- Use a powerful arm drive
- Do not sink into the hips

Sets and reps
3 sets of 4 reps with a 30-second recovery between each rep and a 2-minute recovery between each set. Players to swap roles after each rep.

Variations/progressions
- Both players perform the drill laterally, with one player leading and the other trying to mirror
- Players to perform the drill with one player following the other at the same distance apart. The player who is following calls for the front player to turn and throws them the ball to catch, then the drill is reversed

DRILL HANDWEIGHT DROPS

Aim
To develop explosive power, re-acceleration and, specifically, a powerful arm drive.

Area/equipment
Indoor or outdoor area. Handweights (2–4lb). Position a marker at the start, a second 15 yards away, and a final one 10 yards away from the second.

Description
Players, holding the weights, accelerate to the second marker, where they release the handweights, keeping a natural flow to their arm mechanics. Players continue to accelerate to the third marker before decelerating and walking back to the start, then repeating the drill.

Key teaching points
- Maintain correct running form and mechanics
- Do not stop the arm drive to release the weights
- Keep the head tall
- Quality not quantity is vital

Sets and reps
3 sets of 4 reps with a 3-minute recovery between each set.

Variations/progressions
- On the release of the handweights the coach can call a change of direction – i.e. the player is to accelerate off at different angles
- Perform the drill backwards over the first 15 yards then turn, accelerate and release the weights to explode away
- Perform the drill laterally over the first 15 yards then turn, accelerate and release the weights to explode away
- On the release of the handweights the ball is thrown for the player to accelerate to and catch

DRILL PARACHUTE RUNNING

Aim

To develop explosive running over longer distances (sprint endurance) and explosive acceleration.

Area/equipment

Indoor or outdoor area, 4 markers and a parachute. Mark out a grid of 50 yards in length, place one marker down as a start marker, and 3 further markers at distances of 30 yards, 40 yards and 50 yards from the start marker.

Description

Wearing the parachute, players accelerate to the 40-yard marker then decelerate.

Key teaching points

- Maintain correct running form and mechanics
- Do not worry if the wind and the resistance cause you to feel as though you are being pulled from side to side; this will in fact improve your balance and co-ordination
- Do not lean into the run too much
- Quality not quantity is vital

Sets and reps

3 sets of 5 reps plus 1 contrast run with a walk-back recovery between each rep and a 3-minute recovery between each set.

Variations/progressions

- Explosive re-acceleration using the parachutes' release mechanism; players accelerate to the 30-yard marker, release the parachute and explode to the 40-yard marker before decelerating
- Random change of direction – the coach stands behind the 30-yard marker and, as players release the parachute, the coach indicates a change in the direction of the run; when mastered, the coach can then introduce the ball for players to run onto during the explosive phase
- Coach introduces a cricket ball for players to run onto during the explosive phase
- When the above drill is mastered the ball can be fed in by the coach to encourage the player to accelerate onto a moving ball

DRILL *BALL DROPS*

Aim
To develop explosive reactions.

Area/equipment
Indoor or outdoor area. 1 or 2 tennis balls

Description
Work in pairs; one player drops the ball at various distances and angles from his or her partner. The ball is dropped from shoulder height and immediately the partner explodes forwards and attempts to catch the ball before the second bounce. (Distances between players will differ because the height of the bounce will vary depending on the ground surface.)

Key teaching points
- Work off the balls of the feet, particularly prior to the drop
- Use a very explosive arm drive
- The initial steps should be short, fast and explosive
- At the take-off do not jump, dither or hesitate
- Work on developing a smooth one-movement run

Sets and reps
3 sets of 10 reps with a 2-minute recovery between each set.

Variations/progressions
- Player to hold 2 balls and to drop just 1
- Work in groups of 3 with 2 of the players at different angles alternately dropping a ball for the third player to catch; on achieving this, the player turns and accelerates away to catch or dive on the second ball.
- Alter the start positions, e.g. sideways, backwards with a call, seated etc.

DRILL BREAK-AWAY MIRROR

Aim
To develop multi-directional explosive reactions.

Area/equipment
Indoor or outdoor area. 1 Break-Away Belt.

Description
Work in pairs and face each other attached by the Break-Away Belt. Set a time limit. Player 1 is the proactive player while Player 2 is reactive. Player 1 attempts to get away from Player 2 by using either sideways, forwards or backwards movements. Players are not allowed to turn round and run away. The drill ends if and when the proactive player breaks the belt connection or the time runs out.

Key teaching points
- Stay focused on your partner
- Do not sink into the hips
- Keep the head tall and the spine straight
- Maintain correct arm mechanics

Sets and reps
3 sets where 1 set = 30 seconds of each player taking the proactive role followed by a 1-minute recovery.

Variations/progressions
Side-by-side mirror drills – the object is for the proactive player to move away laterally and gain as much distance as possible before the other can react.

DRILL MEDICINE BALL (JELLY BALL) WORKOUT

Aim
To develop explosive upper-body and core power.

Area/equipment
Indoor or outdoor area. Jelly Balls of various weights can be used.

Description
Working in pairs, the players perform simple throws, e.g. chest passes, single arm passes, front slams, back slams, twist passes, woodchopper and granny throws.

Key teaching points
- Start with a lighter ball for a warm-up set
- Start with simple movements before progressing to twists etc.
- Keep the spine upright
- Take care when loading (catching) and unloading (throwing) as this can put stress on the lower back

Sets and reps
1 set of 12 reps of each drill with a 1-minute recovery between each drill and a 3-minute recovery before the next exercise.

Variations/progressions
- Front slam
- Back slam
- Woodchopper
- Chest pass
- Single arm thrust
- Side slam

Front slam

Back slam

Woodchopper

Chest pass

Side slam

Single arm thrust

DRILL   SLED RUNNING

Aim
To develop explosive sprint endurance.

Area/equipment
Large outdoor grass area. Markers and Sprint Sled. Mark out a distance of 30–60 yards.

Description
The player is connected to the sled and sprints over the nominated distance before recovering, turning round and repeating the drill.

Key teaching points
- Maintain correct running form and mechanics
- Maintain a strong arm drive
- Often players will need to use an exaggerated lean to initiate the momentum required to get the sled moving
- As momentum picks up, the player should transfer to the correct running position

Sets and reps
2 sets of 5 reps plus 1 contrast run with a 1-minute recovery between each rep and a 3-minute recovery between each set.

Variation/progression
5-yard explosive acceleration – the player covers 50 yards by alternating between acceleration and deceleration phases over distances of 5 yards. (NB: Quality not quantity is the key here!)

DRILL *PLYOMETRICS – LOW-IMPACT QUICK JUMPS*

Aim
To develop explosive power for running, jumping and changing direction.

Area/equipment
Indoor or outdoor area. Fast Foot Ladder or markers placed 18 inches apart.

Description
The player performs double-footed single jumps, i.e. 1 jump between each rung (see Fig. 5.6(a)). On reaching the end of the ladder, the player turns round and jumps back.

Key teaching points
- Maintain correct jumping form and mechanics
- The emphasis is on the speed of the jumps, but do not lose control, i.e. avoid feeling as though you are about to fall over the edge of a cliff when you reach the end of the drill
- Do not lean forwards too much

Sets and reps
2 sets of 2 reps with a 1-minute recovery between each set.

Variations/progressions
- Backwards jump
- Two jumps forwards and one back (see Fig. 5.6(b))
- Sideways jumps
- Sideways jumps, two forwards and one back
- Hopscotch – 2 feet in the square and then 1 foot either side of the next square
- Left- and right-footed hops
- Increase the intensity – replace ladders or markers with 7–12 inch hurdles and perform the drills above.

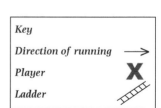

Key
Direction of running →
Player X
Ladder

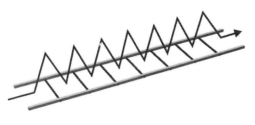

Figure 5.6(a) Low-impact quick jumps

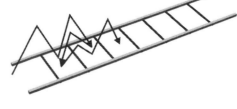

Figure 5.6(b) Low-impact quick jumps – 2 forward and 1 back

DRILL PLYOMETRIC CIRCUIT

Aim
To develop explosive multi-directional speed, agility and quickness.

Area/equipment
Indoor or outdoor area. Place ladders, hurdles and markers in a circuit formation as shown in Fig. 5.7.

Description
The players are to jump, hop and zigzag their way through the circuit as stipulated by the coach.

Key teaching points
- Maintain the correct mechanics for each part of the circuit
- Ensure that there is a smooth transfer from running to jumping movements and vice versa

Sets and reps
5 circuits with a 1-minute recovery between each circuit.

Variations/progressions
Work in pairs. Player 1 completes the circuit while Player 2 feeds the ball in at various points around the circuit for Player 1 to pass back.

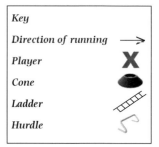

Key	
Direction of running	$\longrightarrow$
Player	X
Cone	
Ladder	
Hurdle	

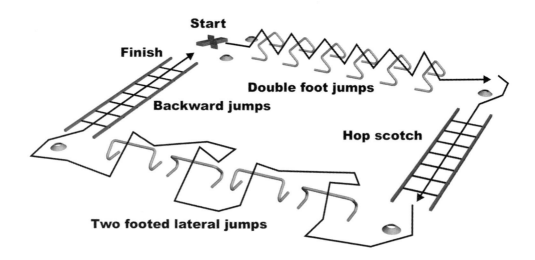

Figure 5.7 Plyometric circuit

DRILL PLYOMETRICS – DROP JUMPS

Aim
To develop explosive multi-directional speed.

Area/equipment
Indoor or outdoor area with a cushioned or grassed landing surface. A stable platform or bench to jump from of variable height (15–36 inches), depending on the stage in the season.

Description
The player stands on the platform and jumps off with feet together, lands on the balls of the feet then accelerates away for 5 yards.

Key teaching points
- Do not land flat-footed
- Do not sink into the hips on landing
- Maintain a strong core
- Keep the head up – this will help align the spine

Sets and reps
2 sets of 10 reps with a 3-minute recovery between each set.

Variations/progressions
- Backwards drop-jumps
- Side drop-jumps
- Drop-jumps with a mid-air twist
- Include a ball for the players to accelerate on to

This stage is quite short in duration, but very important, bringing together all the elements of the continuum into a highly competitive situation involving other players. Short, high-intensity tag-type games and random agility tests work well here.

The key is for players to be fired up and to perform fast, explosive and controlled movements that leave them exhilarated, as well as mentally and physically ready for the next stage in training or the next game.

DRILL *BRITISH BULLDOG*

Aim
To practise multi-directional explosive movements in a pressured situation.

Area/equipment
Outdoor or indoor area of approximately 20 square yards and about 20 markers to mark out start and finish lines.

Description
One player is nominated and stands in the centre of the grid, while the rest stand to one side. On the coach's call all the players attempt to get to the opposite side of the square without being caught by the player in the middle. When the player in the middle captures another player, she or he joins them in the middle and helps to capture more 'prisoners'. See Fig. 6.1.

Key teaching points
- Use correct mechanics at all times
- Keep head and eyes up to avoid collisions with other players

Sets and reps
Play British Bulldog for approximately 3–4 minutes before moving on to the more technical aspects of the game.

Variation/progression
The player in the middle uses a tennis ball to touch other players in order to capture them. The ball can be held or thrown.

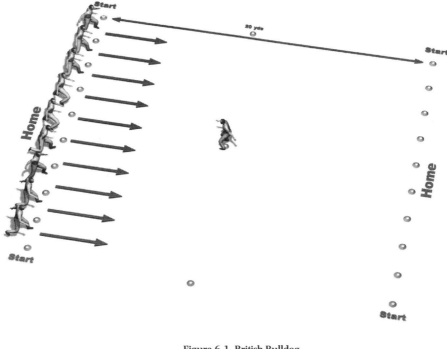

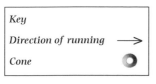

Key	
Direction of running	→
Cone	◎

Figure 6.1 British Bulldog

DRILL CIRCLE BALL

Aim
To practise using explosive evasion skills.

Area/equipment
Outdoor or indoor area. Mark out a circle about 15 yards in diameter (depending on the size of the group). Tennis balls.

Description
One or two players stand in the centre of the circle while the players on the outside have 1 or 2 balls. The object is for those on the outside to try and make contact (with the ball) with those on the inside. The players on the inside try to dodge the balls. The winners are the pair that has the least number of hits during their time in the centre. See Fig. 6.2.

Key teaching point
Players on the inside should use correct mechanics.

Sets and reps
Each pair to stay in the centre area for 45 seconds.

Variations/progressions
Players in the middle have to hold on to each other's hand or use a Break-Away Belt.

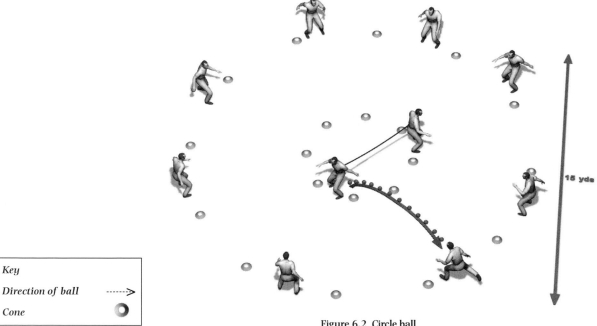

Key

Direction of ball ------>

Cone

Figure 6.2 Circle ball

DRILL ROBBING THE NEST

Aim
To practise multi-directional explosive speed, agility and quickness.

Area/equipment
Outdoor or indoor area with an outer circle measuring 25 yards in diameter, and a centre circle measuring 2 yards in diameter marked out with markers. Place a number of balls in the centre circle.

Description
Two nominated players defend the 'nest' of the cricket balls with the rest of the players standing on the outside of the area. The game starts when the outside players run in and try to steal the cricket balls from the nest, then run to the outside of the circle, the safe zone. The two defenders of the nest try to prevent the robbers from getting the cricket balls to the safe zone by tagging them or getting in their way. For every successful tag and prevention, the ball is returned to the centre circle. See Fig. 6.3.

Key teaching points
- Correct mechanics must be used at all times
- Players should dodge, swerve, weave, sidestep etc.
- Light contact only should be used

Sets and reps
Each pair to defend for about 45 seconds.

Variations/progressions
Attackers work in pairs: one attempts to retrieve the ball from the middle by getting to the ball and rolling it out for the outer partner to field.

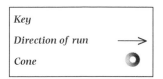

Key	
Direction of run	→
Cone	◎

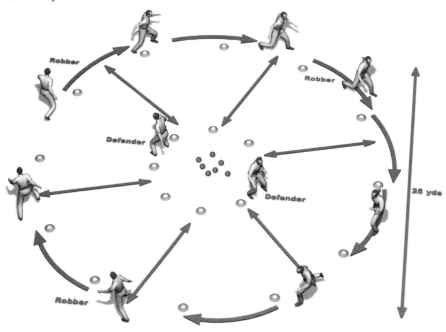

Figure 6.3 Robbing the nest

123

DRILL ODD ONE OUT

Aim
To practise speed, agility and quickness in a competitive environment.

Area/equipment
Outdoor or indoor area; markers and cricket balls. Mark out an outer circle of 20–25 yards in diameter and a centre circle of about 2 yards in diameter.

Description
Place a number of cricket balls in the centre area, one fewer than the number of players present. The players are situated on the outside of the larger circle. On the coach's call the players start running round the larger circle. On the coach's second call they collect a ball from the centre circle as quickly as possible. The player without a ball is the odd one out and performs a cricket skill drill as directed by the coach. The coach then removes another ball and repeats the process. See Fig. 6.4.

Key teaching points
- Correct mechanics must be used at all times
- Players should be aware of other players around them

Sets and reps
Play the game until a winner emerges.

Variations/progressions
Work in pairs joined together by holding hands or using the Break-Away Belt, with one ball between 2 players. If they break away from each other, they are disqualified.

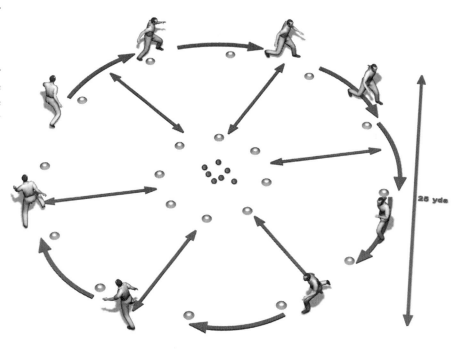

25 yds

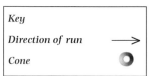

Key	
Direction of run	→
Cone	●

Figure 6.4 Odd one out

DRILL *MARKER TURNS*

Aim
To practise multi-directional speed, agility and quickness.

Area/equipment
Outdoor or indoor area of about 20 square yards. 50 small markers. Place the markers in and around the grid; 25 of the markers should be turned upside down.

Description
Working in two small teams (2–3 players), one team attempts to turn over the upright markers and the other team attempts to turn over the upside-down markers. The winners are the team that has the largest number of markers their way up after 60 seconds. See Fig. 6.5.

Key teaching points
- Initiate good arm drive after turning a marker
- Use correct multi-directional mechanics
- Be aware of other players around the area

Sets and reps
A game should last for 60 seconds.

Variations/progressions
Use 4 teams and allocate 4 sets of different-coloured markers.

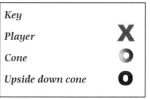

Key	
Player	**X**
Cone	O
Upside down cone	**O**

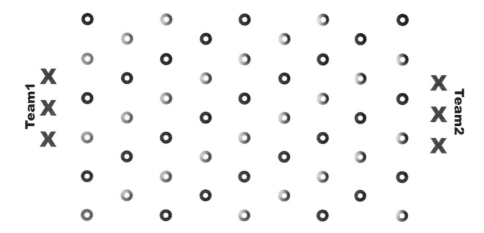

Figure 6.5 Marker turns

CHAPTER 7 POSITION-SPECIFIC DRILLS

This section provides examples not just of cricket-specific but also of position-specific patterns of movement. It looks at combining all the areas of the SAQ Continuum – including techniques, equipment and drills – into games and position-specific situations to improve and perfect the movement skills required by players for optimal performance.

The primary aim is to improve the multi-directional explosive speed, agility, control, power and co-ordination required by cricket players in all areas of the pitch. These drills are best introduced when the foundation work of SAQ Training has been mastered and during training sessions where attention is being given to position-specific movements.

POSITION-SPECIFIC – BATSMAN

DRILL   *EXPLOSIVE FOOT SPEED AND REACTION*

Aim
To develop explosive quick feet for batting either on the front or back foot.

Area/equipment
Indoor or outdoor area, Side-Stepper and cricket ball.

Description
Batsman wearing Side-Stepper adjusted so that the cord is shortened between the ankles performs front-foot shots for 15 seconds, then removes the Side-Stepper and performs the same drill immediately afterwards (contrast phase) for 5–10 seconds. Repeat for the required sets.

Key teaching points
- Work off the balls of the feet
- Use quick, powerful foot movements
- Do not sink into the hips
- Use correct batting technique as prescribed by the coach
- Keep the head still at all times

Sets and reps
4 sets of 15 seconds plus contrast drill.

Variations/progressions
- Back-foot shot
- Place markers around the front, sides and back of the batsman; the coach nominates a marker, the batsman moves his/her feet to the marker and plays the required shot

POSITION-SPECIFIC – BATSMAN

DRILL ## RESISTED RUNNING BETWEEN WICKETS

Aim

To develop acceleration, explosive turning and reacceleration for running between the wickets.

Area/equipment

Indoor or outdoor area, wicket or 22-yard marked-out grid, Viper Belt.

Description

Batsman 1 stands on the crease. Player 2, who is attached to the safety harness, begins to walk down the centre of the wicket (see Fig. 7.1(a)); after 3–4 yards the batsman accelerates with overspeed assistance down the wicket. Batsman 1 passes Player 2 and accelerates towards the other end of the wicket, now beginning to be resisted by the Flexi-cord. Player 2 turns and begins to move in the opposite direction (see Fig. 7.1(b)). Batsman 1 is now pulled again with overspeed back to the wicket for the second run. As the batsman grounds his bat, Player 2 will have begun to walk back to the starting position, therefore providing the second stage of resistance prior to the end of the run. The action is best described as a whiplash motion with Player 2 controlling the handle and the batsman at the end of the line.

Key teaching points

- Maintain correct running form and mechanics
- Use short steps prior to and after the turn
- Do not lunge at the crease

Sets and reps

3 sets of 3 runs with one contrast at the end of each set; a 30-second recovery at the end of each run and a 2-minute recovery at the end of each set.

Variations/progressions

Vary starting positions, e.g. side-on.

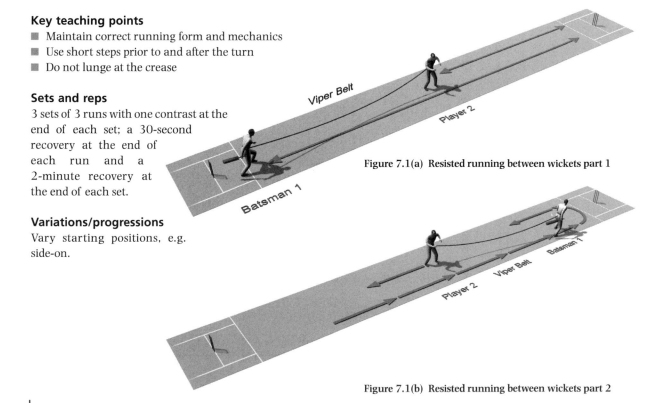

Figure 7.1(a) Resisted running between wickets part 1

Figure 7.1(b) Resisted running between wickets part 2

AGILITY DISC BATTING

Aim
To develop balance, co-ordination and proprioreception.

Area/equipment
Indoor or outdoor area, 2 Agility Discs and a cricket bat.

Description
Batsman to stand on agility discs and play different shots while trying to balance and control his/her body.

Key teaching points
- Stay strong in the core
- Do not sink in the hips
- Keep the head still

Sets and reps
1 minute on, 30 seconds off, 1 rep of 30-second recovery. Repeat 10 times.

Variations/progressions
Introduce a ball for the player to hit.

DRILL — *BATTING WITH A REACTOR BALL*

Aim
To develop eye–hand and eye–foot co-ordination, explosive reactions and anticipation to cope with quick changes of direction.

Area/equipment
Indoor or outdoor area, Reactor ball and cricket bat. N.B. Ball works best on a hard indoor or outdoor surface.

Description
Two batsmen work together: Batsman 1 tosses the ball for Batsman 2 to play shots. The ball can be tossed at different heights, which causes different bounces. Ball to played not on the full.

Key teaching points
Maintain correct posture at all times.

Sets and reps
10 sets of 6 balls with a 30-second recovery between each set.

Variations/progressions
Batsman 1 to alternate from Reactor Ball to a normal ball to add confusion.

POSITION-SPECIFIC – BATSMAN

DRILL *SHORT, FAST FOOT LADDER WITH ANKLE WEIGHTS*

Aim
To develop explosive and controlled quick feet.

Area/equipment
Indoor or outdoor area. Short, 7.5-foot Fast Foot Ladder, 1 set of 1-kilo ankle weights and a cricket bat.

Description
Batsman attaches ankle weights then performs a number of fast foot drills down the short ladder for no more than 30 seconds per drill. The ankle weights are then removed and the drill repeated (contrast phase) for 10 seconds.

Key teaching points
- Maintain correct running form
- Use short, sharp, explosive steps
- Work on the balls of the feet
- Keep the head still
- Keep the core strong

Sets and reps
5 sets of 30-second reps and one contrast.

Variations/progressions
- Perform drill with handweights
- Perform drill attached to Viper Belt

POSITION-SPECIFIC – BATSMAN
WEIGHTED BAT

Aim
To develop upper-body strength and power.

Area/equipment
Indoor or outdoor area. Cricket bat can be weighted by strapping ankle weights around the blade of the bat.

Description
Player plays normal shots with the weighted bat.

Key teaching points
- It is important to follow sets and reps closely
- Always perform a contrast shot

Sets and reps
6 sets of 8 shots, 1 minute rest between each set.

Variations/progressions
- Vary sets and reps
- Vary the weight on the bat

POSITION-SPECIFIC – BOWLER
DRILL RESISTED BOWLING

Aim
To develop explosive power for bowling.

Area/equipment
Indoor or outdoor area. Viper Belt, cricket ball and a set of stumps.

Description
Work in pairs: Bowler 1 wears the Viper Belt, Bowler 2 holds the Flexi-cord. Bowler 1 starts to run 3–4 yards from the bowling crease and bowls in his/her normal fashion. Bowler 2 holds the Flexi-cord and provides resistance. On completing 6 resisted balls, Bowler 1 performs 2 unresisted.

Key teaching points
- Maintain correct running form mechanics
- It is important not to sink into the hips
- Maintain strong core
- Perform a normal follow-through

Sets and reps
3 sets of 6 balls and 2 contrast balls, with a 15-second recovery between each ball and a 2-minute recovery between each set.

Variations/progressions
- Bowler 2 sits down to provide resistance from a lower angle
- Add an additional Flexi-cord to increase resistance

DRILL ASSISTED RESISTED TOW RUNS

Aim
To develop an explosive run-up and power for bowling.

Area/equipment
Indoor or outdoor area. Viper Belt, wicket and cricket ball.

Description
Bowlers 1 and 2 are attached to one another by the Viper Belt. Bowler 1 runs away from Bowler 2, who stands still until pulled forward. Bowler 1 has the ball in his/her hand and attempts to run and bowl in a normal fashion, while being resisted from behind by Bowler 2. See Fig. 7.2.

Key teaching points
- Maintain correct running form and mechanics
- Both bowlers should use strong arm drive
- Both bowlers should use short steps during the acceleration phase
- Bowler 2 must keep an upwards and forwards lean and not try to resist the acceleration by leaning backwards

Sets and reps
2 sets of 6 reps, bowler to take 30 seconds recovery between each set and 2 minutes recovery between each rep.

Variation/progression
Bowler 2 to run with handweights.

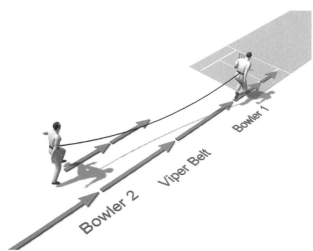

Figure 7.2 Assisted resisted tow runs

POSITION-SPECIFIC – BOWLER

DRILL SIDE-STEPPER BOWLING

Aim
To develop explosive running and vertical take-off at the bowling crease.

Area/equipment
Indoor or outdoor area. Wicket, cricket ball and Side-Steppers.

Description
Bowler wears the Side-Stepper and performs a normal bowling run-up and delivery.

Key teaching points
- Maintain correct running techniques
- Attempt to maintain normal stride pattern and take-off

Sets and reps
2 sets of 6 reps, with a walk-back recovery after each set and a 2-minute recovery between each rep.

Variations/progressions
- Vary reps and sets
- Alternate run with high-knee skips

DRILL *BOWLING SPEED DEVELOPMENT*

Aim

To increase rotational speed of arm so that the bowler can bowl faster.

Area/equipment

Indoor or outdoor area. Wall or net, 1-kilo Jelly Ball, foam ball and cricket ball.

Description

The bowler bowls with his/her normal action using a 1-kg Jelly Ball either to a partner, against a wall or into a net. There is no need for the bowler to complete a full run-up – they can take 1 or 2 steps then bowl. After bowling the required number of times with the Jelly Ball, use the foam ball and repeat: this is the contrast phase. Due to the lightness of the foam ball, the rotational speed of the arm will be quicker. Finally, the foam ball is replaced by the standard cricket ball, which is once again bowled the required number of times.

Key teaching points

- Maintain a strong core at all times
- Maintain correct bowling technique at all times

Sets and reps

3 sets of 4 reps with the Jelly Ball, 2 with the foam ball and 2 with the standard cricket ball, with a 1-minute recovery between each set.

Variations/progressions

Vary sets and reps of all the different balls.

DRILL

POSITION-SPECIFIC – BOWLER
EXPLOSIVE DELIVERY STRIDE DEVELOPMENT

Aim
To develop explosive power throughout the delivery stride.

Area/equipment
Indoor or outdoor area. Cricket wicket and Sonic Chute.

Description
Bowler performs his/her normal run-up to the crease while wearing the Sonic Chute. Just before delivery, the chute is released. The bowler will shoot forwards, which is when the ball should be delivered.

Key teaching points
- Maintain correct running form and mechanics
- Practise releasing the Sonic Chute
- Do not worry if, with the wind and the resistance, you feel as though you are being pulled from side to side: this will improve your balance and co-ordination
- Do not lean into the run too much
- Quality not quantity is important

Sets and reps
3 sets of 6 reps plus 1 contrast, with a walk-back recovery between each rep and a 3-minute recovery between each set.

Variations/progressions
Coach to introduce a change of direction after the ball has been delivered.

POSITION-SPECIFIC – WICKETKEEPER
LATERAL POWER AND SPEED DEVELOPMENT

Aim

To develop explosive, controlled lateral ability and precise and accurate catching of the ball at speed under pressure.

Area/equipment

Indoor or outdoor area. Viper Belt with 2 Flexi-cords (1 attached at each side), stumps, two 7.5-foot Fast Foot Ladders and a cricket ball.

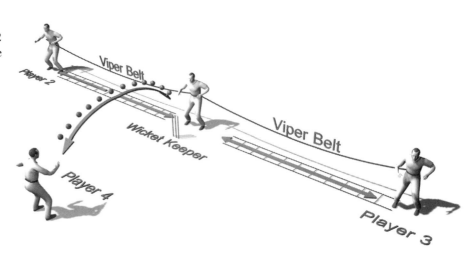

Description

Wicketkeeper 1 is connected to Players 2 and 3 by the Viper Belt and 2 Flexi-cords. The ladders are placed 1–2 yards behind the stumps laterally on each side, leaving a gap for Wicketkeeper 1 to stand in. Wicketkeeper 1 stands behind the stumps and in between the 2 ladders, while Players 2 and 3 provide resistance from both sides. Player 4 stands in front of the wicket and throws or bounces cricket balls to each side of the wicket; Wicketkeeper 1 moves laterally down the ladders under resistance from one side and catches the ball. The ball is returned to Player 4 and the drill is repeated. On completing the required number of reps, the Viper Belt is removed and the drill is performed without resistance (contrast phase). See Fig. 7.3.

Key teaching points

- Reassert good arm mechanics when possible
- Maintain correct running form
- Use correct technique for catching and throwing

Sets and reps

3 sets of 8 reps plus 2 contrast, with a 3-minute recovery between each set.

Variations/progressions

- Can be performed without the ladders
- Work in the sandpit or use high-jump landing mats so that the wicketkeeper can dive
- Wicketkeepers to wear full kit at all times

Figure 7.3 Lateral power and speed development for wicketkeepers

| DRILL | *VERTICAL POWER* |

Aim

To develop vertical take-off power for the production of more air time and height when jumping to catch the ball.

Area/equipment

Indoor or outdoor area, about 3–4 square yards. 1 Viper Belt with 2 Flexi-cords and a cricket ball.

Description

Work in groups of 4 with 1 player wearing the Viper Belt, which has 1 looped Flexi-cord attached on each side. Players 2 and 3 stand a yard away, one either side of the resisted player; they stand on the Flexi-cord with their legs approximately 1 yard apart. The fourth player stands in front of the resisted player and throws the ball above their head. The resisted player jumps to catch the ball before regaining position to repeat the drill.

Key teaching points

- Maintain correct jumping form and mechanics
- Do not sink into the hips either before take-off or on landing
- Work off the balls of the feet
- On landing, regain balance before the next jump
- Practise perfect timing of the jump

Sets and reps

3 sets of 8 reps plus 1 contrast jump, with a 3-minute recovery between each set.

Variations/progressions

Quick jumps – i.e. no repositioning between jumps. These are fast, repetitive jumps performed as quickly as possible.

DRILL **EXPLOSIVE GROUND REACTIONS**

Aim
To develop multi-directional explosive movements.

Area/equipment
Indoor or outdoor hard-surfaced area. Reactor ball.

Description
Wicketkeepers work in pairs or individually against a wall. The Reactor ball is thrown to land within 1 yard of the wicketkeeper, who attempts to catch it before the second bounce. Due to the shape of the ball it will bounce off the surface at different angles and different heights, forcing the wicketkeeper to react accordingly.

Key teaching points
- Bend at the knees, not at the waist
- Work off the balls of the feet
- Keep the hands in front of the body ready to react
- The ball should not be thrown hard – it will do the necessary work itself

Sets and reps
3 sets of 25 reps with a 1-minute recovery between each set.

Variations/progressions
Vary the starting position of the wicketkeepers e.g. backwards, sideways etc.

POSITION-SPECIFIC – WICKETKEEPER
DRILL | *EXPLOSIVE LATERAL MOVEMENT DEVELOPMENT*

Aim
To develop explosive, co-ordinated and controlled lateral movement. To increase foot speed and improve foot-to-ground contact.

Area/equipment
Indoor or outdoor area. Two 7.5-feet Fast Foot Ladders and a Side-Stepper.

Description
The Fast Foot Ladders are placed laterally in a straight line one after the other with a 1-yard gap between them. The wicketkeeper, wearing the Side-Stepper adjusted so that the Flexi-cord is shorter between the ankles, stands in the central gap between the ladders. Player 2 stands 5 yards in front and throws cricket balls to the left and right of the wicketkeeper who, using short, explosive steps, moves laterally down the ladders to catch and return the balls.

Key teaching points
- Work off the balls of the feet
- Use strong arm and knee drive
- Try to keep a rhythmic skip
- Keep the head up, maintaining a good posture
- Use correct throwing and catching skills at all times

Sets and reps
3 sets of 6 reps with a 30-second recovery between each rep and a 2-minute recovery between each set.

Variations/progressions
Player 2 uses 2 balls; after throwing the first ball, the wicketkeeper moves across to catch the second ball thrown to the other side.

POSITION-SPECIFIC – WICKETKEEPER
DRILL *FAST FEET EYE–HAND CO-ORDINATION*

Aim
To develop lightning-fast feet and eye–hand co-ordination simultaneously.

Area/equipment
Indoor or outdoor area. Sidestrike and a cricket ball.

Description
Wicketkeeper performs lateral footwork patterns on the Sidestrike while catching and returning the ball thrown by Player 2.

Key teaching points
- Work off the balls of the feet
- Maintain a strong core
- Keep the hips square
- Develop a rhythm
- Use correct catching and throwing techniques

Sets and reps
5 sets of 30 seconds with a 45-second recovery in between and a 3-minute recovery after all sets have been completed. NB: this is a very high-intensity drill.

Variations/progressions
Vary the footwork patterns.

CHAPTER 8 VISION AND REACTION

It is assumed by many involved in cricket who have 20/20 vision that their visual ability for the sport will be competent. Most eye tests give us results only for static visual acuity, that is the ability to identify certain black letters on the white background of an eye chart. Cricketers use a whole range of visual abilities whenever decisions need to made and movements into areas need to be completed, particularly when catching or stopping a cricket ball.

The following drills will help in the areas of:

Dynamic visual acuity – the ability to maintain the clarity of an object while moving.

Colour vision – simply to recognise the various colours of the spectrum.

Depth perception – the ability for a cricketer to judge distances rapidly and accurately.

Visual reaction time – the time required for a cricketer to perceive and respond to visual stimulation.

Central-peripheral awareness – the ability of cricketers to pay attention to what they are looking at, yet to be aware of what is going on peripherally around them without moving their eyes and losing the central focus.

Eye–hand–body co-ordination – the ability to integrate the eyes, hands and body to work as whole unit.

DRILL VISUAL ACUITY EYE–HAND REACTION

Aim

To develop fast, accurate catching skills. To develop the player's visual skills.

Area/equipment

Outdoor or indoor area. Visual Acuity Ring (see Fig. 8.1).

Description

Work in pairs approximately 5 yards apart. The ring is tossed so that it rotates through the air and is caught by the player on the colour nominated by the coach.

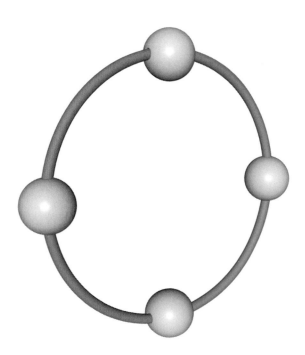

Key teaching points

■ Keep the head still – move the eyes to track the ring
■ Work off the balls of the feet at all times
■ The hands should be out and in front of the body ready to catch the ring

Sets and reps

2 sets of 20 reps with a 1-minute recovery between each set.

Variations/progressions

Turn and catch.

Figure 8.1 Visual Acuity Ring

DRILL   PERIPHERAL AWARENESS

Aim
To develop peripheral awareness. To help the player to detect and react to the ball coming from behind and from the side more quickly.

Area/equipment
Outdoor or indoor area. Peripheral Vision Stick (see Fig. 8.2).

Description
Work in pairs with Player 1 behind Player 2, who stands in a ready position. Player 1 holds the stick and moves it from behind Player 2 into their field of vision. As soon as Player 2 detects the stick, he or she claps both hands over the ball at the end of the stick.

Key teaching points
- Player 2 should work off the balls of the feet and in a slightly crouched position with the hands held out ready
- Player 1 must be careful not to touch any part of Player 2's body with the stick
- Player 1 should vary the speed at which the stick is brought into Player 2's field of vision

Sets and reps
2 sets of 20 reps with no recovery between each rep and a 1-minute recovery between each set.

Variations/progressions
Instead of using a vision stick, throw balls from behind Player 2, who has to fend them off.

Figure 8.2 Peripheral Vision Stick

DRILL   REACTOR BALL

Aim
To develop lightning-quick reactions.

Area/equipment
Outdoor or indoor area but not a grass surface. Reactor ball or rugby ball.

Description
Work in pairs, standing 5 yards apart. The ball is thrown so that it lands in front of the player; because of the structure of the ball it will bounce in any direction. The player has to react and catch the ball before it bounces for a second time.

Key teaching points
- The player catching the ball should work off the balls of the feet and in a slightly crouched position with the hands out ready
- The ball should not be thrown hard – it will do the necessary work itself

Sets and reps
2 sets of 20 reps with no recovery between each rep and a 1-minute recovery between each set.

Variations/progressions
- Work individually or in pairs by throwing the ball against the wall
- Stand on agility discs while throwing the ball to each other

DRILL | *BUNT BAT*

Aim
To develop lightning-quick hand–eye co-ordination.

Area/equipment
Outdoor or indoor area. Bunt Bat (see Fig. 8.3) and tennis balls or bean bags.

Description
Work in pairs with one of the players holding the Bunt Bat. The partner stands about 3–4 yards away and throws a ball or bean bag, simultaneously calling the colour of the ball on the Bunt Bat. The player's task is to fend off the ball/bean bag with the appropriate coloured ball on the Bunt Bat.

Key teaching points
▪ Start throwing the balls/bean bags slowly, and gradually build up speed
▪ The player with the bat should be in a get-set position

Sets and reps
3 sets of 25 reps with a 30-second recovery between each set.

Variations/progressions
▪ Use different coloured balls/beans bags – when the ball/bean bag has been thrown, it is to be fended off with the corresponding coloured ball on the Bunt Bat
▪ The player with the bat stands on an agility disc while performing the drill

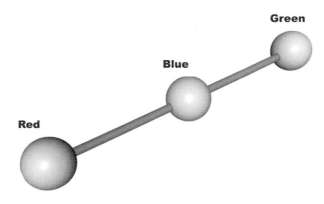

Figure 8.3 Bunt Bat

DRILL   FOLLOW THE THUMB

Aim
To develop all-round and peripheral vision.

Area/equipment
Indoor or outdoor area.

Description
Hold one hand out in front and make the 'thumbs up' sign. Keeping your head still and moving only your eyes, move the thumb up, down and around, making sure you are moving to the extremes of your range of vision. Start slowly and increase the speed of the movement.

Key teaching points
▪ Sit or stand upright with good posture
▪ Try the drill with both hands
▪ Keep the head still
▪ Move only your eyes

Sets and reps
5 sets of 1-minute reps with a 30-second recovery between each set.

Variations/progressions
While performing the drill, get another player to toss you a ball to catch and return (one in each set).

DRILL   *TRACKING AND FOCUS*

Aim
To develop ball-tracking ability and to make subtle focus adjustments.

Area/equipment
Indoor or outdoor area. Cricket ball.

Description
Draw numbers and letters on 4 sides of the ball – use black ink on white balls, and white ink on red balls. Two players stand 10–15 yards apart. Player 1 holds up the ball for 2 seconds so that a number is clearly facing Player 2. Player 2 calls out the number as the ball is thrown to be caught. The drill is now reversed.

Key teaching points
- Keep the head still
- Move the eyes, not the head

Sets and reps
5 sets of 12 reps with a 30-second recovery between each set.

Variations/progressions
- Vary the time the ball is held up for
- Vary the distance
- Vary the angle

DRILL FAST HANDS

Aim
To develop lightning-quick hand reactions.

Area/equipment
Indoor or outdoor area.

Description
Working in pairs, Player 1 puts their hands together and holds them slightly away in front of the chest. Player 2 stands directly in front with their hands held at their sides. The drill begins with Player 2 attempting to slap Player 1's hands. Player 1 tries to prevent Player 2 by moving the hands away as quickly as possible. Players alternate.

Key teaching points
- Stand in an athletic position
- Keep the head still

Sets and reps
30 seconds each per drill.

Variations/progressions
- Player 1 holds the hands out with the palms facing the ground and the tips of the thumbs just touching. Player 2 holds the hands just above. The drill commences with Player 2 attempting to slap both hands before Player 1 can react by moving them away.
- Player 1 stands directly in front of Player 2, 1 or 2 yards away. Player 1 jabs a punch at Player 2, who attempts to clap both hands over the fist.

CHAPTER 9 CRICKET–SPECIFIC WEIGHTS PROGRAMME

The following cricket-specific weights programme is ideal for all playing positions and can be implemented both pre- and in-season. It is simple, basic and time efficient, and has been developed to improve whole-body muscular strength and dynamic explosive power. There is a focus on core stabilisation and upper body proprioception, including functional and cricket-specific movements.

It is simple to implement; you don't need to attend a gym or depend on machines and an array of weights. All you need is a set of adjustable dumb bells (5 kg to 12 kg per bell), a 55 or 65 cm core stability ball and a 5 kg jelly ball. The equipment is easily transportable and fits into the boot of a car, so can be transported to away games.

The object of the programme is to slightly increase the weight lifted when the number of reps is lower, so that the next time you perform a higher number of reps you will be lifting more weight. The programme sheet can be copied so you can monitor your lifts in the space provided. Work to failure, then recover and begin the next set without compromising good technique.

Before beginning the programme, warm up and mobilise your body by completing a set of the exercises with no or very light weights; this will prepare your body for the hard work to come.

Complete the programme at least twice a week, preferably when fresh. You can use some of your 'free' time during games, for example a high order batsman who is out early should have time to complete the 30–35 minute session before fielding. Also included are drill descriptions and teaching points for all exercises.

DRILL CORE BALL DUMBBELL PRESS (1A)

Description
Stabilise yourself on the core ball. Press the dumbbells overhead, then lower. Maintain the tempo of 4 seconds down, 2 seconds up.

Key teaching points
- Maintain a strong base; tighten your core muscles and maintain throughout the exercise
- Keep your hips up and squeeze your gluteal muscles throughout
- Maintain a smooth, continuous action
- Do not lock out your elbows
- Remember to breathe out on the effort

DRILL HAND-CLAP PRESS-UP (1B) – COMPLEX

Description
Get into a press-up position. Lower your chest to the floor then push back explosively.

Key teaching points
- Try to maintain good body alignment throughout
- Make sure you cushion your impact and get back into the correct start position between each rep

DRILL SINGLE-LEG DUMBBELL SQUAT (2A)

Description

Holding a dumbbell in each hand, perform a single-leg squat.

Key teaching points

- Maintain balance and stability throughout
- Look ahead and focus
- Keep your back straight and your core muscles tight
- Remember to breathe out on the effort

DRILL SINGLE-LEG JUMP CATCH (2B)

Description

Perform single-leg jumps on alternate legs, while your partner throws you a ball to catch in the 'up' position.

Key teaching points

- Maintain balance and stability throughout
- Keep your back straight and your core muscles tight

DRILL   *CORE BALL UPRIGHT PRESS (3A)*

Description

Stabilise yourself on the core ball. Press the dumbbells overhead then lower, maintaining the tempo of 4 seconds down to 2 seconds up.

Key teaching points

- Maintain a good base; tighten your core muscles and maintain throughout the exercise
- Maintain a smooth, continuous action
- Do not lock out your elbows
- Remember to breathe out on the effort

DRILL   *CORE BALL JELLY BALL THROW (3B) – COMPLE.*

Description

Stabilise yourself on the core ball. Press the ball over your head using an explosive action, using a wall to rebound the ball.

Key teaching points

- Maintain a good base throughout; tighten your core muscles and maintain throughout the exercise
- Control each throw

DRILL ANGLED DUMBBELL LUNGE (4)

Description
Stand upright with your feet shoulder width apart and knees slightly bent. Holding the dumbbells at your sides, lunge forward with alternate legs so that your knee bends to a 45 degree angle.

Key teaching points
- Maintain good posture and alignment throughout the exercise
- Control the lunge on the way down, then 'snap' back to the start position

DRILL CORE BALL SINGLE-ARM BENT-OVER ROW (5)

Description
Stabilise yourself on the core ball with a dumbbell in one hand. Pull the dumbbell into your side, leading with the elbow, then lower. Alternate your arms.

Key teaching points
- Keep your back straight and tighten your core muscles throughout
- Do not twist
- Keep your head up
- Maintain a smooth, continuous action

WEIGHTS PROGRAMME

EXERCISE ORDER		Session 1	Sesssion 2	Session 3
1A Core ball dumbbell press	**Weight**			
	Sets & Reps	3 × 8	3 × 7	3 × 6
	Speed	4 down 2 up	4 down 2 up	4 down 2 up
	Recovery	30 sec	30 sec	30 sec

After each set of reps move immediately to next drill within the specified time. Return to commence next s

1B Hand-clap press-up	**Weight**			
	Sets & Reps	2 × 8	2 × 7	2 × 6
	Speed	N/A	N/A	N/A
	Recovery	2 min	2 min	2 min
2A Single-leg dumbbell squat	**Weight**			
	Sets & Reps	3 × 7 × 7	3 × 8 × 8	3 × 9 × 9
	Speed	4 down 2 up	4 down 2 up	4 down 2 up
	Recovery	30 sec	30 sec	30 sec

After each set of reps move immediately to next drill within the specified time.

2B Single-leg jump catch	**Weight**			
	Sets & Reps	3 × 5 × 5	3 × 6 × 6	3 × 4 × 4
	Speed	N/A	N/A	N/A
	Recovery	2 min	2 min	2 min
3A Core ball upright press	**Weight**			
	Sets & Reps	3 × 9	3 × 8	3 × 7
	Speed	4 down 2 up	4 down 2 up	4 down 2 up
	Recovery	1 min	1 min	1 min

After each set of reps move immediately to next drill within the specified time.

3B Core ball jelly ball throw	**Weight**	5 kg	5 kg	5 kg
	Sets & Reps	3 × 10	3 × 8	3 × 6
	Speed	N/A	N/A	N/A
	Recovery	2 min	2 min	2 min
4 Angled dumbbell lunges	**Weight**			
	Sets & Reps	3 × 6 × 6	3 × 8 × 8	3 × 10 × 10
	Speed	control down, quick back		
	Recovery	2 min	2 min	2 min
5 Core ball single-arm bent-over row	**Weight**			
	Sets & Reps	3 × 8 × 8	3 × 10 × 10	3 × 8 × 8
	Speed	4 down 2 up	4 down 2 up	4 down 2 up
	Recovery	3 min	3 min	3 min

Session 4	Session 5	Session 6	Session 7	Session 8	Session 9	Session 10
3 × 7	3 × 8	3 × 9	3 × 7	3 × 6	3 × 7	3 × 6
4 down 2 up	4 down 2 up	4 down 2 up	4 down 2 up	4 down 2 up	4 down 2 up	4 down 2 up
30 sec	2 min	2 min	2 min	2 min	2 min	2 min
2 × 7	2 × 8	2 × 9	2 × 7	2 × 6	2 × 7	2 × 6
N/A	N/A	N/A	N/A	N/A	N/A	N/A
2 min	2 min	2 min	2 min	2 min	2 min	2 min
× 5 × 5	3 × 6 × 6	3 × 7 × 7	3 × 9 × 9	3 × 5 × 5	3 × 8 × 8	3 × 6 × 6
4 down 2 up	4 down 2 up	4 down 2 up	4 down 2 up	4 down 2 up	4 down 2 up	4 down 2 up
30 sec	30 sec	30 sec	30 sec	30 sec	30 sec	30 sec
3 × 6 × 6	3 × 7 × 7	3 × 5 × 5	3 × 8 × 8	3 × 7 × 7	3 × 9 × 9	3 × 7 × 7
N/A	N/A	N/A	N/A	N/A	N/A	N/A
2 min	2 min	2 min	2 min	2 min	2 min	2 min
3 × 10	3 × 12	3 × 10	3 × 8	3 × 10	3 × 12	3 × 8
4 down 2 up	4 down 2 up	4 down 2 up	4 down 2 up	4 down 2 up	4 down 2 up	4 down 2 up
1 min	1 min	1 min	1 min	1 min	1 min	1 min
5 kg	5 kg	5 kg	5 kg	5 kg	5 kg	5 kg
3 × 8	3 × 12	3 × 10	3 × 8	3 × 12	3 × 10	3 × 8
N/A	N/A	N/A	N/A	N/A	N/A	N/A
2 min	2 min	2 min	2 min	2 min	2 min	2 min
3 × 7 × 7	3 × 6 × 6	3 × 8 × 8	3 × 9 × 9	3 × 10 × 10	3 × 7 × 7	3 × 8 × 8
control down, quick back			control down, quick back			
2 min	2 min	2 min	2 min	2 min	2 min	2 min
3 × 7 × 7	3 × 9 × 9	3 × 10 × 10	3 × 12 × 12	3 × 8 × 8	3 × 9 × 9	3 × 8 × 8
4 down 2 up	4 down 2 up	4 down 2 up	4 down 2 up	4 down 2 up	4 down 2 up	4 down 2 up
3 min	3 min	3 min	3 min	3 min	3 min	3 min

CHAPTER 10 WARM-DOWN AND RECOVERY

Due to the intense activity levels achieved during the main part of the session, time should be allowed for players to reduce the heart rate gradually to near resting levels. This will help to:

- disperse lactic acid

- prevent blood pooling

- return the body's systems to normal levels

- assist recovery

The structure of the warm-down is essentially the reverse of the Dynamic Flex warm-up, and should last for approximately five minutes depending on the fitness levels of the players. The warm-down should begin with a selection of moderate Dynamic Flex movements; the warm-down should then become less intense and smaller in amplitude. The exercises should still focus on quality of movement (good mechanics).

Static stretches should be incorporated following this stage of the session. Players should perform stretches that mirror the movements carried out in the warm-down.

See Chapter 1 for details of the drills you can choose for the warm-down, remembering to reverse the order of the movements performed and to pick drills that reflect the activities carried out in the rest of the session.

CHAPTER 11 SAQ CRICKET PROGRAMMES

This chapter provides sample training sessions and programmes for both professional and amateur teams, with a focus on in-season sessions.

The art to any programme is how it is periodised throughout the year, plus its ability to recognise individual needs and provide individual leeway for unscheduled changes. The best programmes are those that have variation, provide challenges, keep the players on their toes and accept individuality. Too much of the same demotivates individuals and teams, and performance, both individual and team, may be compromised.

Some simple rules

- Start with Dynamic Flex

- Explosive work and sprints should be completed early in the session before any anaerobic work

- Plan sessions so that an explosion session is followed by a preparation day

- Progress from simple to complex drills

- Don't restrict programmes to one-week periods; work with different blocks of 4–8–10–12 days

- Teach or learn one new skill a day

- Rest and recovery periods should be well planned

- Vary work/rest ratios

- Build up strength before performing plyometrics

- Keep sessions short and sharp; explanations and discussions should be conducted before and afterwards, not in activity time

- Finish off sessions with static (PNF) stretching

Pre–season

Mention the words 'pre-season training' to most players and you will get a look of horror. For years coaches and trainers have been fixated by the development of the aerobic energy system by utilising long, slow, steady-state runs from 5 miles to anything up to 8 miles.

Research clearly states that this type of activity is not suitable for cricket players and is more likely to make them slower and cause unnecessary injuries.

Most activity in cricket is for a very short duration. Cricket is a start–stop game that utilises fast-twitch muscle fibres and depends primarily on the anaerobic system. By training the anaerobic system a number of benefits are gained that impact on the overall level of cricket fitness:

- An increased ability to tolerate higher levels of lactate, a metabolic by-product that causes muscular fatigue if it is not dispersed

- An increase in aerobic power, the energy system that uses oxygen without turning off the fast twitch fibres, which are vital because they enable cricket players to perform explosive, multi-directional movements such as sprinting, jumping, diving and turning

- An improved recovery time – this is very important and enables cricket players to perform at a high intensity and to then recover more quickly for the next activity

It is quite simple: long, slow runs do not represent what happens on the field of play – they are not cricket-specific. Intermittent, intensive runs of various work/rest ratios including side-step runs, swerves, backward runs and jumps prepare players better for the demands of the game.

Therefore, pre-season professional programmes should start with a higher percentage of time spent on running mechanics than explosive work. As the season draws closer, the programmes' emphases should progressively change, with a higher percentage of time being spent on the explosive development and less on the mechanics.

Once the season has started, you can follow the in-season programmes (amateur or professional) outlined in this chapter.

IN–SEASON PROGRAMME: AMATEUR

Amateur teams normally train 2–3 times a week depending on the standard of the league they play in. The SAQ Cricket Programme can make training not only interesting and challenging, but also great fun, with the added bonus of good results.

Don't fall into the trap of steady-state runs even at amateur level: interval running and SAQ drills will make your players fitter and faster.

All sessions start with Dynamic Flex

SUNDAY	Rejuvenate/pool recovery	
MONDAY	**SAQ Session** Cricket skills Interval sprints Vision work	90 mins
TUESDAY	Individual strength and power programme	40 mins
WEDNESDAY	**SAQ Session** Cricket skills Strength/power work Vision work	90 mins
THURSDAY	Individual circuit conditioning	40 mins
FRIDAY	Combination Dynamic Flex warm-up Cricket skills	75 mins
SATURDAY	Warm-up, **game**, cool-down, refuel	

IN-SEASON PROGRAMME: PROFESSIONAL

Due to the unpredictable nature of cricket it is impossible to provide a standardised programme of training. The successful method of training in cricket in-season is to provide the players with a menu of drills to be performed within the week. This will then enable players with different roles within the team, e.g. an opening bowler who may sit in the pavilion for a day and half, while their team-mate batsmen score runs, to maintain and develop the skills relevant to their positions.

MENU

1	Dynamic Flex before each game or session	15 mins each session
2	2 sessions of sprint endurance	25 mins each session
3	3 SAQ Combination work, ladders, hurdles	15 mins each session
4	2 explosion sessions (use short reps and sets)	15 mins each session
5	2 weight-training sessions	35 mins each session
6	Vision work, every day	10 mins each session
7	Flexibility work, 3 times a week	10 mins each session
8	Swimming, 2–3 times a week	15 mins each session

NB: Bowlers should perform Dynamic Flex before every bowling session both before and within a game.

Glossary

Acceleration Increasing velocity, specifically over the first 25 yards.

Aerobic Energy system that uses oxygen.

Agility The ability to move quickly in any direction and maintain balance.

Anaerobic Energy system that does not rely on oxygen to function.

ATP **A**denosine **TriP**hosphate. The only source of energy that muscle can utilise. All food gets broken down into this molecule.

Competitive skills Skills such as running, jumping or lateral movements that can be used in the sporting environment.

Contrast A stage after that of resistance where the player/athlete performs the same drill but is unresisted.

Dorsiflexion Flexing the ankle by lifting the toes, as if one were trying to lift up a bucket with one's toe.

Dynamic Any movements, particularly those involving stretches, that actively move a limb through its full range of motion.

Explosive The ability to generate great amounts of force in a very short space of time.

Fast-twitch fibres Present in larger proportions in muscles of explosive/power athletes, enabling them to perform explosive, powerful movements, as opposed to endurance athletes who possess a greater number of slow-twitch muscle fibres.

Flexibility Range of motion about a joint. Also the ability of a joint to be elongated.

Force application Ability to generate the summation of synchronised force to be applied at a specific point in time or space, e.g. when throwing a ball.

Goal-setting An important part of mental preparation in which one thinks about and decides what one wants to achieve.

Hops Single-leg repeated jumps.

Jumps Double-leg repeated jumps.

Lactate Leftover by-product of anaerobic metabolism that is converted back into ATP by the liver.

Maximum speed Fastest speed obtainable by an individual, usually achieved between 30 and 50 yards.

Muscular efficiency The use of stores of muscle energy in a manner that is not wasteful to the athlete, through minimising and eliminating wasted movements.

Neuromuscular recruitment Activities that work to activate more muscle units.

Peripheral vision Visual ability to see things or movements while focusing on another object.

Plantar flexion Pointing the toes downwards from the ankle, i.e. full extension of the ankle.

Plyometrics Any activity that utilises the stretch reflex eliciting rapid changes between eccentric and concentric contractions.

PNF Proprioceptive Neuromuscular Facilitation is a form of training that improves flexibility by increasing the strength of the agonist/primary muscle while decreasing the resistance of the antagonist.

Power output The rate at which work is done.

Progressive overload In training, the concept that one needs constantly to force the body to adapt to new stresses.

Proprioception One's ability to adjust to any stimulus. Can be applied directly to or around the body.

Quicken To generate a movement in a shorter space of time.

Resistance A type of training that involves tools to increase the force required to move.

Specificity Training precisely for the demands of your sport or skill development.

Speed The ability to move fast over a specific distance.

Strength The raw ability to overcome gravitational or applied forces.

References

Bennett, S., (1999) 'New Muscle Research Findings', Muscle Symposium, AIS, Canberra, Australia

Gleim, G. W. and McHugh, M. P., (1997) 'Flexibility and Its Effects on Sports Injury and Performance', *Sports Medicine*, 24(5): 289–99

Hennessy, L. Dr, (2000) 'Developing Explosive Power', Paper, SAQ Symposium, June 2000

Herbert, R. D. and Gabriel, M., (2002) 'Effects of stretching before or after exercising on muscle soreness and risk of injury: a systematic review', *The British Medical Journal*, 325: 468–70

Kokkonen, J., Nelson A. G. and Cornwell, A., (1998) 'Acute muscle stretching inhibits maximal strength performance' *Research Quarterly for Exercise and Sport*, 4: 411–15

Pope, R. C., (1999) 'Skip the Warm-up', *New Scientist*, 18 Dec. 164(2214): 23

Oberg, B., (1993) 'Evaluation and improvement of strength in competitive athletes' in K. Harms-Ringdahl (ed.) *Muscle Strength* (Edinburgh: Churchill Livingstone), 167–85

Smythe, R., (2000) 'Acts of Agility', *Training and Conditioning*, 5(4): 22–5

Index of drills